Eduardo Manuel Gil

Hispano Aviación HA-1112

Bf 109s Made In Spain

- The Last Survivors Of The Mythical Saga

Dedicated to:
Solete (mi vida)
Mis padres Salud y Eduardo.
Merce, Caco y Ricardo.
Ángel y sus nietos June, Iñigo e Ibón.
A mis abuelos Mercedes, Salud, Mami, Manuel y Juan.

Acknowledgments for their invaluable help in bringing this work to fruition: Juan Arráez Cerdá (without his help this text never come true), Marisol García Gómez, Ricardo Ramallo Gil, Giuseppe Guiduccio, Fernando Salobral, Asisbiz, Warbirds, Aviationcorner.net, Ricardo Sanabria, Juan M. González, Fernando Llorente, José A. Rubio, J.M. Ochoa Cao and Francisco Andreu (generous Aviation lovers).

KAGERO

MORE FROM KAGERO

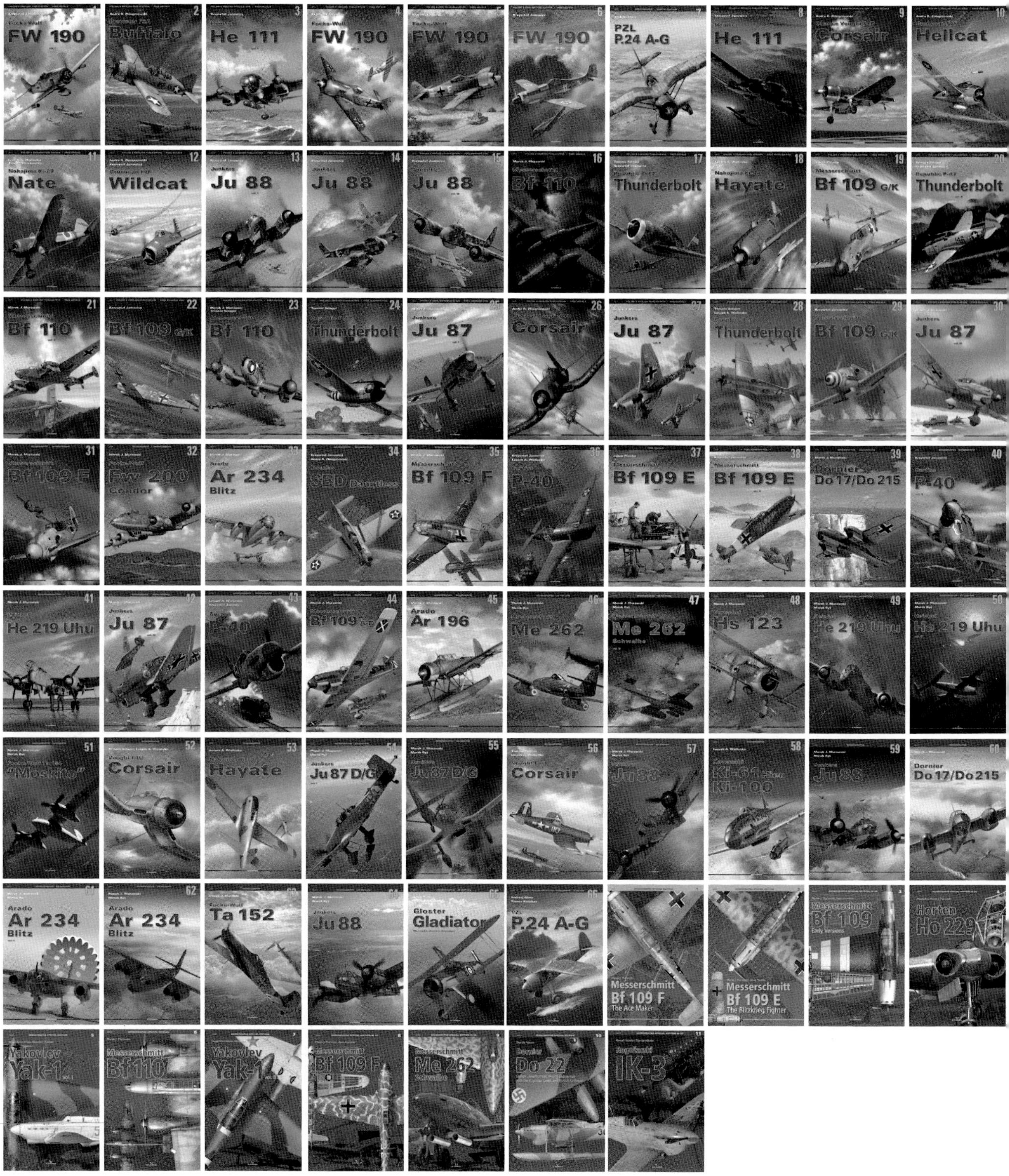

Hispano Aviación HA-1112. Bf 109s Made In Spain – The Last Survivors Of The Mythical Saga • Eduardo Manuel Gil Martínez • First edition • LUBLIN 2019

• Printed in Poland • **ISBN 978-83-66148-33-8**

Editing: **Eduardo Manuel Gil Martínez** • Translation: **Ricardo Ramallo Gil** • Cover artwork: **Christian Zambruno** • Color profiles: **Arkadiusz Wróbel** • Photos: **Eduardo M. Gil Martínez, Public Domain, Asisbiz, Francisco Andreu via Juan Arráez, Juan Arráez Cerdá, Juan Arráez by SHYCEA, Juan M González, Warbirds, José A. Rubio via J M. González, JM Ochoa via JM González, Ricardo Sanabria** • Design: **KAGERO STUDIO**

KAGERO Publishing
Akacjowa 100, Turka, os. Borek, 20-258 Lublin 62, Poland, phone/fax: (+48) 81 501 21 05
www.kagero.pl • e-mail: kagero@kagero.pl, marketing@kagero.pl
w w w . k a g e r o . p l
Distribution: **KAGERO Publishing**

Introduction

Dear reader, in this text we will try to remember the fabulous history of Messerschmitt Bf 109s made in Spain, which gave rise to two models of aircraft such as HA-1109 and HA-1112, with its consequent subvariants. Thanks to the tenacity and the need of the Spanish Government to have combat aircraft, it was possible to maintain on the first line until 1965 an airplane whose origin was 30 years earlier.

It is a recognized fact that the Messerschmitt Bf 109 fighter was one of the first modern fighters, in addition to having the honor of being the fighter built in greatest number in all history (reaching almost 35000 units without counting their Spanish derivatives). Its good flight performance gave it the opportunity to fight in the skies of Europe during World War 2 (WW2) being the spearhead of the German fighter for several years (in conjunction with the Focke Wulf Fw 190) thanks to the continuous updates that kept it in production until the end of the war (being one of the aircraft that more air victories accumulated during its operational use getting to be a dangerous rival for the Spitfire and Hurricane during the Battle of Britain in the Bf 109 E version, or the whip of the Soviet skies with the Bf 109 F, or being a worthy rival against aircraft as powerful as the Mustangs and Thunderbolt with the versions Bf 109 G and Bf 109 K) and subsequently continued in service until well into the 50s in countries like Romania (until Moscow decided to avoid the presence of fighters of German origin in the Romanian air force), Switzerland or Finland. Another important fact was the reuse of airframes of the Bf 109 that had been built during WW2 by Germany and that were becoming scrap in countless scrapyards throughout Germany; to this group belong the Czechoslovak Bf 109s (S 99). But three new aircraft based in the Bf 109 were manufactured in Spain that enlarged the Bf 109 life about 20 years. They will be as we can see throughout these pages, the Bf 109 Spaniards who continued in active service until 1965 coexisting with the 2nd and the 3rd jet generation first aircraft.

Beginning the story from the start, it is mandatory to remember that the Bf 109first prototype, the Bf 109 V1 flew in May 1935, powered by a Rolls Royce Krestel engine. Its creator was Willy Messerschmitt in collaboration with Walter Rethel, a design engineer from the Plow factory. Before starting to deep inside our text, it is important to remember that the Bf 109s were originally manufactured by Willy Messerschmitt at the Bayerische Flufzeugwerke, so these superb fighters were officially baptized with the abbreviation Bf until 1938, which began to be called acronyms Me. The change of initials was motivated by the great prestige of the German engineer who had created the aircraft. In this text, we will refer to Bf 109 or Me 109, as Bf 109 since the aircraft arrived in Spain in 1936 when still Willy Messerschmitt was not yet the owner of the Bayerische Flugzeugwerke.

Three Messerschmitt Bf-109 B-2 belonging to the Legion Condor. These early models of the famous German fighter used by the Spaniards during the Spanish Civil war, made it easier for Spaniards to learn how to handle more modern models such as the E or F. [Courtesy of Asisbiz]

The new German fighter came after the request of the German Air Ministry (RLM) of a high-performance modern fighter to replace the Luftwafe German fighters fleet as the Heinkel He 51 and Arado Ar 68. This design arose after a contest held by the RLM and it did not take time to the Bayerische Flugzeugwerke to start making improved versions of the Bf 109. Among its first versions, the Bf 109B, C and D models stood out, which would soon be used in combat.

The flights of the first prototypes of Bf 109; the V1, V2 and V3, were made between May 1935 and May 1936. Just a couple of months later the Spanish Civil War (SCW) broke out in Spain, and the similar ideology of the rebel side with the German government led to Germany's decision to try in authentic combat conditions the new Luftwaffe jewel. Thus, at the end of 1936, three of the ten built prototypes were sent to Spain experimentally (among them the model Bf 109 V4, with Jumo 210 A engine of 610 HP, two machine guns Rheinmetall MG-17 in the wings of 7, 9 mm and a 20 mm MG/FFM cannon, which fired through the propeller hub); to those who would join during the first months of the following year the airplanes of the series B (Bf 109 B). The German support to the rebellious side in the Spanish Civil War was very important in all aspects, but with regard to air warfare, materialized in the so-called "Legion Condor". Specifically, in the "Condor Legion" Jagdgruppe 88 that was where the Bf 109s were deployed, forming the first operational squadrons with the production Bf 109B.

The arrival of new Bf 109 occurred steadily, and not only from the initial B model, but from the more modern models C and D. Obviously the German aid to the National side (insurgents) materialized in the "Legion Condor" was very important , but also the Germans obtained a great information of the behavior of the Bf 109 in combat and therefore of the possible im-

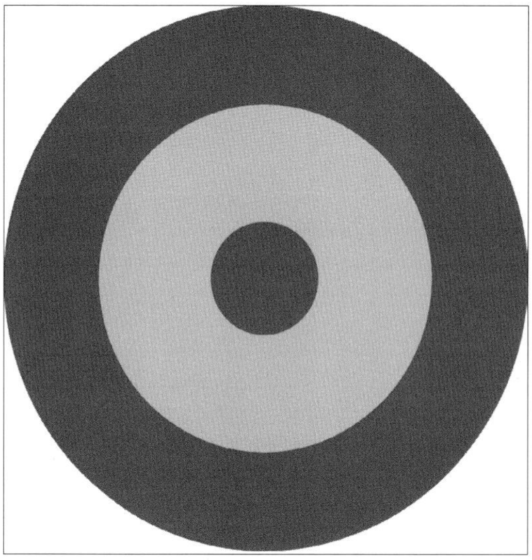

Spanish Air Force badge, showing the colors of the Spanish flag: a circle with the three colors of the Spanish national flag: red in the outside ring-yellow in the middle ring-red in the inner disc. [Public domain by DV Wiebe]

provements that had to be made to him. The learning of the Luftwaffe in the SCW not only to the development of this particular plane, but to the tactics of air war in general.

Although the Bf 109s were fighting in Spain, even these planes did not do it with the Spanish national badge since they belonged to the Luftwaffe. The interest of the National side in the acquisition of these modern airplanes fructified when from 1938 they began these airplanes to happen at the hands of Spanish pilots flying in the 6 Fighter Group. The Germans did not raise objections to the sale of the airplanes, already that they were already working on the development of the new version of Bf 109, the Bf 109 E (which was the main German fighter at the beginning of WW2).

Following the history of the Bf 109 in Spain, in April 1938, five Bf-109 C (equipped with an injection engine and armed with four machine guns) arrived at the Tablada airfield in Sevilla (Seville in English) and in August the most modern ones began to arrive. Bf-109 D (equipped with carburetion engine and armed with four machine guns). The Tablada aerodrome together with its neighbour El Copero aerodrome, will witness for almost 30 years the flights of the iconic fighter designed by Willy Messerschmitt, from the time of the biplanes to the first supersonic flights.

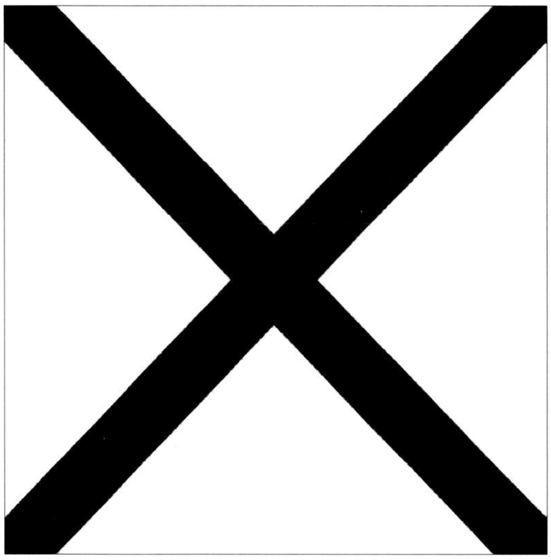

Badge used by the Spanish Air Force aircraft in the tail. Over a white background it was painted a black Burgundy or St. Jacques Cross. This badge still is used nowadays. [Public domain by Kizar]

Spanish aviation after the Spanish Civil War

After the bloody Spanish Civil War that took place between 1936 and 1939, Spain had been exhausted and destroyed after declaring the end of the war on April 1. But due to the war years, it had accumulated a large amount of very heterogeneous war material. Regarding the Air Force (known as National Aviation during the Civil War), we can assure that according to the report sent on February 9, 1940 by the Spanish Air Force general director, it had 1148 aircraft of 95 different models that turned the Spanish Air Force (by number of airplanes) into one of the most numerous in Europe after Germany, Great Britain, France or Italy. The aircraft heterogeneity and the lack of resources led to a high accident rate reaching 105 crew members in the period 1939-1945. At that time, there were more plans than pilots.

The National Aviation (this was the denomination of the Spanish Air Force of the side of the insurgents) received approximately 39 Bf 109 B, five Bf 109 C and 36 Bf 109 D. At the end of the SCW in 1939, the state of conservation in which they were Bf 109 Spaniards was terrible due to the constant use they had. Of the planes received, 9 had been shot down during the war, 26 were retired for various reasons and about 15 were sent to Germany for various repairs. Despite this, from the "Legion Condor" were transferred to Spain 27 Bf 109 in their models A, B, E-1 and E3 (note the modern Bf 109 E in its first versions E-1 and E-3) that were finally deployed within the National Aviation, which shortly after (in October 1939) would be renamed Air Force (Ejército del Aire or EdA or Spanish Air Force), going to 25 Group in Logroño, and fighter schools in Reus and Morón de la Frontera (some Bf 109 of which fought during the SCW remained in flight until 1954). In the Spanish Air Force, the 3 Bf 109 Squadrons coexisted with their old rivals of Soviet manufacture I-15 or I-16, being at the end of 1939 the most modern and powerful fighters that flew in Europe. But in September 1939 the WW2 began and with it the developments and advances in armament technology evolved with such speed, that in just a few months the Spanish Bf 109s had become obsolete before the mass appearance of more modern German fighter models.

But we have to start from the beginning, so on August 8, 1939, the Air Ministry was created,

One of the 36 Bf 109 D that were delivered to National Aviation during the Spanish Civil War. They were numbered from 6-51 to 6-86. They were identified in the Spanish Air Force as C.4; some of these planes remained in flight in the Fighter Group based in Reus until they were discharged in 1954. [By Francisco Andreu via Juan Arráe]

with General Juan Yagüe, a Legion veteran and Germanophile, elected as minister (this election was surprising, since the initial candidate was General Kindelán who had directed the National Aviation during the Civil War, which created some discomfort among the Spanish pilots to feel discriminated). On October 7, 1939 by State´s Headquarters law, the Air Force (EdA) was born. Its assignments included "the fundamental one to develop all its offensive power by means of its air units". On November 9, the Aviation Weapon was created, as the main element and axis of the EdA. On December 15, the Aeronautical Engineers Corps was created within the EdA.

Before his appointment, Yagüe had traveled to Germany as part of the Spanish mission that accompanied the return of the Legion Condor. There, he took the opportunity to learn many details of the Luftwaffe structure and organization, which was the example to be followed by military aviation in Spain. During the 10 months that General Yagüe led the ministry (he was ceased in June 1940 and replaced by Juan Vigón who was not an aviator either), he drew the operational and organizational lines to be followed by the EdA, which was none other than the one of the German Luftwaffe. Although many of Yagüe's ideas were finally fulfilled (his plan marked the development of the EdA in the following years after WW2), one of the illusions that was evidently never fulfilled was getting 5,000 aircraft in the EdA in a time of only 5 years since his arrival at the ministry.

Obviously the conservation and operation state in which these aircraft were found was very different. For this reason, it was necessary to determine which aircraft would be in the inventory of the EdA and which ones could be put up for sale or in some cases, those that would become scrap. In January 1940 the distribution of the Span-

At the end of the Spanish Civil war (SCW), Spain had 14 Messerschmitt Bf 109 A and B. These aircraft were already obsolete at the beginning of WW2. The airplane in the photograph shows the typical Legion Condor badge during the SCW. [Public domain]

ish fighters was as follows (based in José Luis González Serrano work):

Regiment	Group	Base	Aircraft	Number
21	21	Getafe	CR.32	33
21	22	Getafe	CR.32	30
	23	Tablada	CR.32	26
	24	Manises	I-15bis	20
	25	Agoncillo	Bf 109	41
	26	León	CR.32	35
	27	Nador	G.50 , He 112	20
	28	Son San Juan	I-16	11
				216

As it is reasonable to think, the total number of Spanish fighters was 126, but the operative fighters number was lower (161).

Spain during World War 2

The Spanish situation that was decreed at the beginning of the world conflict in September 1939 was neutrality despite the fact that a good part of the Germanophile population existed in Spain; in that decree we can read that "knowing officially the state of war that unfortunately exists between England, France and Poland on one side, and Germany, on the other, is hereby ordered, the strictest neutrality to the Spanish citizen".

After the important Allies defeats against the German Army, on June 12, 1940 Spain went to "non-belligerency" situation, in a similar way to how Italy did before joining the world conflict. Despite the first step that Spain took towards Germany, the negotiations for the entry into the war carried out with Von Ribbentrop did not culminate in the union of Spain with the Axis due to lack of understanding (voluntary or not) on both sides.

The events were developing at great speed in Europe and on June 25, 1940 the armistice came in France. In October 1940 Hitler and Franco met in the French town of Hendaye with the intention that Spain would join Germany in the war (as happened with Mussolini in Bordighera in February 1941), but the Spanish demands prevented the pact. For this reason, the situation in which Spain was facing Germany was quite complex.

It is true, according to Neulen, that Spain was possibly the only country in which a large part of the population saw Germany's attack on the USSR with satisfaction. The Spanish Civil War (SCW) was very recent (it ended on April 1, 1939) and the USSR had helped the defeated side. The winning side (the Nationalists) under Francisco Franco command was clearly opposed to communism and of course to the country that was the communism symbol: the USSR.

The invasion of the Soviet Union decreased the pressure that Adolf Hitler performed on Francisco Franco, by means of the shipment of an expeditionary force to Russia. This step was considered by the Germans at the beginning as a first step for the gradual entry of Spain into the war. Also this troops shipment to integrate in the German Army, would allow them to "pay" indirectly part of the debt contracted by Spain with Germany in concept for the help of Germany in the SCW to the Nationalist band.

It is a known fact, although most of the Spanish population is not familiar with it, the existence of the Spanish Volunteers Division, (popularly known as the Blue Division or División Azul) that emerged as a response to popular clamor on part of the Spanish population that after the German army attack to the USSR in June 1941, showed the desire to fight the Soviets

Due to the great popular enthusiasm that was generated, little effort was necessary to recruit its members among the military and thousands of volunteers who prepared to sign their names in the recruitment offices that were created for that purpose. Among these volunteers, there were some soldiers who had not fought in the Spanish Civil War and wanted to prove to themselves and their comrades that they were capable of going to the front. It is said that some young officers fresh out of the Academy, faced with the war in the world, did not agree to let this opportunity that was presented to them pass by. Also in young university students with a desire for adventure, or with the romantic ideal of defending convictions such as God and Homeland, they strongly grasped the idea of enlisting in the Spanish Volunteers Division that was integrated within the German army with the denomination of Infanterie Division 250 (Infantry Division 250).

As an element of support to the Spanish ground forces, it was decided to also create

Messerschmitt Bf 109 E-3 in San Javier airbase. These aircraft were the most powerful fighters of the Ejército del Aire (Spanish Air Force) so they were intended to protect the border with France. [Courtesy of Juan Arráez Cerdá]

Messerschmitt Bf 109E.3 in El Prat / Barcelona, located there for the defense of the French border. [Courtesy of Juan Arráez Cerdá]

an air unit to accompany them on the battle front. For this reason, an air component corresponding to a Fighter Squadron was created; officially called the Expeditionary Squadron in Russia and popularly known as the Blue Squadron (Escuadrilla Azul). We will see later how the Spanish infantry never received the support of their compatriots from the Blue Squadron, even though that was the intention of the Spanish Government.

We have already commented the political situation of Spain during the years of the WW2, so in this chapter, without further delay, we will narrate the participation of Spanish pilots in the world conflict. The winning side in the SCW commanded by General Franco, was evidently close to the German (after the aid of both Germany and Italy in the Spanish conflict) so after the German invasion of the USSR in 1941, as well as the organization of The Blue Division, the Blue Squadron was also created to provide air support to its Blue Division compatriots who fought in the north of the USSR (a fact that would never come to true since the Spanish air unit remained in central Russia, despite the requests of the Spanish Government to be added to the Blue Division). This decision was made at the last moment as Blue Division initial location was also the Central sector, which caused some upset among the volunteers. The Expeditionary Squadron should be the equivalent of a Luftwaffe Staffel, although it was not like a Staffel in reality.

During the SCW, the National Aviation had learned a lot from its Italian comrades and especially from the Germans. One of the aspects that were assimilated by the newly created EdA to impose them on their Blue Squadron was the rotation of the pilots. The pilots of the Legion Condor were rotated every time period with the intention that the maximum number of pilots could take part in the SCW and therefore accelerate their learning and handling of modern aircraft. In the same way, the Spanish Expeditionary Squadron acted during its participation in WW2 within the Luftwaffe. For this reason we should not really talk about the Blue Squadron, but about the Blue Squadrons, since there were 5 Spanish squadrons that fought in the Russian skies throughout their stay on the Eastern front between September 1941 and March 1944 ap-

Several Bf 109 Es lined up in an airstrip with the Bf 109 E-1 (6-127) in foreground. These fighters together with the Bf 109 Fs were the spearhead of the Spanish Air Force in the 1940s. [By Francisco Andreu via Juan Arráez]

At the Orel airbase we see this Bf 109 F-2 belonging to the 2nd Blue Squadron that has been painted the legend MECHANICAL CABO ZARO! PRESENT !, in honor of Tomas Zaro Rubio, who died on July 28, 1942 when he was hit by the propeller of the 109 he was checking. In the fuselage and next to the Balkenkreuz carries the emblem of the Yoke and the Arrows from the Spanish Falange of the JONS (National Syndicalist Offensive Council Spanish Falange). [Courtesy of Juan Arráez Cerdá]

proximately, every six months a Squadron was relieved with the following one.

The 5 Squadrons operated in the USSR without having any relationship with their comrades in the Blue Division, since their actions were developed in the Army Group Center sector during such important moments as the German offensive on Moscow or the battles of Kharkov, Smolensko and Kursk.

The Spanish Expeditionary Squadrons or Blue Squadrons had the opportunity to fly different aircraft models while fighting in the skies of Russia.

There were six main aircraft models: Messerschmitt Bf 109 E7, Messerschmitt Bf 109 F2, Messerschmitt Bf 109 F4, Focke Wulf Fw 190 A2, Focke Wulf Fw 190 A3 and Messerschmitt Bf 109 G6. All the planes were the same as those used by other units of the Luftwaffe, although it is true that when the Spaniards used the E model, some Luftwaffe units already used the F; or when the Spanish used the F, and some German units used the Fw 190. Only the 1st Squadron, the 2nd Squadron and the 5th Squadron flew the Bf 109s, scoring more than 27 destroyed Soviet planes during their combat period.

The main Bf 109s that were flew by the Spanish pilots were:

Messerschmitt Bf 109 E7: the Spanish pilots of the 1st Squadron managed to adapt more easily to this Bf 109 model since during the SCW it was already used in Spain. In addition the EdA had several Bf 109 E1 and E3, so there were several pilot officers who already knew about the use of the plane.

With the Messerschmitt, the Spaniards had an airplane that could carry out both fighter and escort missions as well as ground attacks.

The E7 was a "long range" version of the E4 (which in turn was a version of the E3 with improved weaponry of Oerlikon MG-FF/M guns in each wing and with a higher rate of fire), with the capacity to mount a 300 liters drop tank.

Flying this fighter, the Spanish pilots belonging to the 1st Squadron destroyed 14 Soviet planes during Oct 1941-Dec 1941.

Messerschmitt Bf 109 F4: Possibly this aircraft valuing its performance and firepower was the best Bf 109 of all the models manufactured (later the models increased their weight with the new engines and weapons systems, reducing their maneuverability). F4 was the F series most used version.

This model of the Bf 109 was used by the Spaniards as a pure fighter, which was for the mission for which they were manufactured. This was the first but not the lasttme that Spanish pilots flew this wonderful fighter.

Flying this fighter, the Spanish pilots belonging to the 2nd Squadron destroyed 13 Soviet planes during Jun 1942-Nov 1942. Then the pilots belonging to the 3rd Squadron shot down several Soviet planes until they changed their Bf 109s for Fw 190s, during Dec 1942- Jul 1943.

Messerschmitt Bf 109 G6: This Bf 109 was the result of Germany's need for aircraft with greater speed to deal with enemy aircraft. The power and speed increase in the Bf 109 resulted in the aircraft being heavier and reducing its maneuverability in order to gain speed and horizontal acceleration. It was the most important Bf 109 version and was made as an armaments platform, being able to install field modifications or "Rüstsätse" in the front aerodromes.

No Soviet planes were shot down by the Spanish pilots during Feb 1944- Mar 1944.

The main info about these planes piloted by Spaniards is:

NAME	SQUADRON	ARMAMENT	ENGINE
Messerschmitt Bf 109 E7	1st	2 20 mm cannons + 2 7.92 mm machine guns	Daimler-Benz DB 601 A 1.175 HP
Messerschmitt Bf 109 F4	2nd y 3rd	1 20 mm cannon + 2 7.92 mm machine guns	Daimler-Benz DB 601 E 1.350 HP
Focke Wulf Fw 190 A3	4th	4 20 mm cannons + 2 7.92 mm machine guns	BMW 801 D-2 1700 HP
Messerschmitt Bf 109 G6	5th	1 30 mm cannon + 2 13 mm machine guns	Daimler-Benz DB 605 A 1.475 HP

Messerschmitt Bf 109 F2/F4: In 1943 a very important fact happened, because 15 Bf 109 F2/F4 fighters (previously used by Luftwaffe units) were purchased from Germany at a price of 202,000 marks per aircraft. Possibly there were 10 model F4 fighters and 5 model F2 fighters all with VDM propellers, although there is not complete evidence of it. At that time, the Bf 109 F model had already been replaced in Germany by the following version, Bf 109 G. The Bf 109 F was denominated in Spain "Zacuto".

As we have said, the 15 planes that Spain bought from Germany were not new, but had already been used previously by the Luftwaffe (according to Lucas Molina Franco), as follow:

- 2 planes with 10 flight hours.
- 2 planes with 50 flight hours.
- 5 airplanes with 60 flight hours.
- 3 planes with 110 flight hours.
- 2 planes with unknown number of flight hours.

In addition, accessories for nine aircraft were also purchased as spare parts.

As an example, it´s known that the Bf 109 F W.N. 7486 with Spanish code number 6-135, was before an aircraft operated by 9./JG54.

These very valid aircraft (they became the best with what the Spanish Air Force could fly during the final years of WW2) were delivered at the French airfield in Villecoubley where they were picked up by Spanish pilots (who had been transferred in a Ju 52 belonging to the EdA and from the Iberia airline). At the same aerodrome, the 15 planes were tested by the 15 Spanish pilots under the command of Lieutenant Colonel Manso on May 15, 16 and 17. Finally, on May 17, 1943, they took off towards Chateaurox, where they only landed 14 Bf 109Fs, since one had to make an emergency landing near Poitiers (the pilot was unharmed) that did not allow the plane to be repaired. From Chateaurox they took off on the 17th with a new stop in Toulouse. On

Commander Javier Murcia, 5th Blue Squadron chief testing one of the Messerschmitt Bf 109 G that they just handed over to replace the Fw 190 A-3 that were flying. [Courtesy of Juan Arráez Cerdá]

One of the Bf 109 F that Germany sold to Spain during the World War 2 pictured in the 1940's. This fighter was the C.4F in the Spanish Air Force but was nicknamed "Zacuto". [By Francisco Andreu via Juan Arráez]

the 18th they took off from Toulouse, making a stopover at the Reus Air Base (in Tarragona, near the Pyrenees) on 19th. Subsequently, they continued their flight to the south, stopping on 21st at the Barajas airbase (in Madrid) to continue the fly to their destination: the Morón aerodrome (in Sevilla) where the 14 Bf 109Fs landed on May 22. Although initially they were deployed in the Tablada airbase (Sevilla) along the 22nd Fighter Regiment to help the pilots belonging to the last two Blue Squadrons to fly aircrafts similar to those that could be used in Russia. Initially they remained in Luftwaffe desert scheme camouflage with a solid line demarcation low on the fuselage and Spanish badges in six positions (over and under the wings and in both parts of the fuselage). As all the EdA aircraft, the Bf 109 Fs had white rudder with St. Andrew cross superimposed (a black cross).

The codes were two numbers ahead of and behind the Spanish roundel on the fuselage

Because of its importance in the history of the Spanish Bf 109s, we will remember that Tablada Airbase was used from 1915-16 as a military airfield, although previously it had already been used for the first aviation party (Airshow) that took place in Spain in 1910. In 1920 Tablada became the Air Base in Sevilla, which was inaugurated by King Alfonso XIII on April 16, 1923. During the Spanish Civil War Tablada played an important role, since it was the aerodrome where the Italian planes arrived and were repaired. It was also used during the airlift by which Spanish troops moved from North Africa to the Iberian peninsula at the beginning of Spanish Civil War.

Later (in 1945) the Bf 109 F2 / F4s would be transferred to the 23rd Fighter Regiment in Reus, closer to the French border. There these

Aerial view of the Tablada airbase in Seville in 1928. In this airbase during WW2 the 2nd and 3rd Blue Squadrons pilots were trained; a few years after was one of the airbases where the Buchones were based. Today it is still a military base of the Spanish Air Force. [Public domain]

aircraft nicknamed "Zacutos" were numbered from 6-132 to 6-145. Later the Bf 109 F2 / F4s changed the desert camouflage for a three colors splinter camouflage, remaining the white rudder with the St Andrew cross superimposed.

The Spanish Bf 109 F were mainly deployed in Reus until 1956, when at the beginning of March the 23rd Fighter Regiment became 23rd Group after a new restructuring in the Spanish Air Force. Already at that time the "Zacutos" hardly flew due to the shortage of fuel and because they were very weary.

The Bf 109 Fs received in the Spanish Air Force the denomination C.4 F.

The final blow to the "Zacutos" was the expected arrival of made in USA combat aircarft, which left them relegated to become completely useless, and therefore were immediately scrapped. Except some Bf 109 Fs that were delivered to the Maestranza in Albacete in June 1955, the other "Zacutos" were destroyed to take advantage of the aluminum with which they were manufactured.

Spanish fighter force post WW2

While the acquisition of the Bf 109 F was advancing, the Spanish Government was already trying in 1942 to obtain the construction license of the Messerschmitt Bf 109 G-2 from Germany. With this improved version of the fighter created by Willy Messerschmitt, Spain was trying to modernize its aviation at that time when even the German Reich was the owner of much of Europe. Under the agreements, Germany undertook to send 25 disassembled Bf 109 G-2 that would serve as a reference to Spanish engineers. Although the events did not occur as we can think, since important setbacks appeared in order to the Bf 109 J (the Spanish produced version of the Messerschmitt Bf 109 was to be designated in this way) would fly; although on the other hand it motivated that a new airplane was born, successor of the Bf 109 G as we will tell in the following pages.

At the end of WW2 Spain was in a very difficult situation, because the hard task of rebuilding the country after the Spanish Civil War and the general shortage, we must add the international isolation and economic blockade to which Spain was doomed.

Faced with the inability to keep active the aircraft that had been used until the end of WW2 (see book by the same author "Spanish Air Force during World War II, Germany's hidden ally?") It was decided in the Air Ministry that the Bf 109 should be kept in service as fighters, the He 111 as bombers and reconnaissance and the Ju 52 as transports.

The Bf 109s that Spain owned from the Spanish Civil War, were old models B, C and D with Jumo Junkers engines aircraft named in the Spanish Air Force C-4 (which were definitively retired on July 23, 1955); some weary model E Bf 109 with engine DB named in the Spanish Air Force C-5 and later C.4E (they were definitively retired on July 23, 1955, when the last Emil flyable was delivered to the Maestranza de Logroño) and the Bf 109 F denominated in the Spanish Air Force C-10 (and later C.4F).

Determined to improve Spain's defensive capacity on an individual basis, the plan to put the Spanish Bf 109 G-2 in flight began. The prob-

The aircraft chosen to test the HS12-Z89 engine was the Bf 109E-1 (6-119) belonging to the 23rd Fighter Regiment 25 Group based in Reus. This picture was taken in Reus airbase where the aircraft tests began. [Courtesy of Juan Arráez]

Another picture where we can see how it was necessary to slightly redesign the nose of the Bf 109 E-1 to achieve the right matching of the HS12-Z89 engine. With this aircraft there were no previous tests in wind tunnels, so the engineers did their best. This picture was taken in Reus airbase where the aircraft tests began. [Courtesy of Juan Arráez]

At the end of World War 2, in Czechoslovakia, they were manufactured by the Avia Catowice aircraft with DB-605 engine and Bf 109 G14 fuselage; aircraft with DB-605A engine and Bf 109 G12 fuselage (two crew) and aircraft with Junkers Jumo 211 F engine and Bf 109 G14 fuselage. The first ones were called S-99, the second CS-99 and the last S-199. In the picture an israeli Avia S-199 June 1948. [Public Domain]

lems with the licensed manufacturing of the Bf 109 G-2 did not take long to appear because the components for the manufacture of the first 25 airplanes had to arrive in Spain in two shipments by train; however, only the first shipment arrived in Spain. In the first shipment the airframes of the airplanes were received, but in the second shipment that never arrived in Spain were the tail entanglements, wings, engines, and armament.

On the never received content of the second shipment from Germany have been mainly two theories, although currently the first one is discarded and the second fully confirmed.

The first theory, now discarded, places us in the difficulties that the German Reich had for the control of the occupied Europe skies and the Reich itself. The bombings against the German industry and infrastructure were showing that the war sooner or later would end with the defeat of Germany. For that reason, before the great effort of the German war industry (there is some version that suggests that the pressure that the Allies towards the Spanish government, increased the German distrust towards Spain) could not or did not want to supply the engines Daimler Benz DB 605A promised. This situation caused the Spaniards Bf 109 G-2 to be built but the engines were not available for them, so they had to look for alternatives to put the aircraft in flight.

The other version is supported by the great Spanish experts in the Bf 109s and their Spanish derivatives, Carlos Pérez San Emeterio and José Luis González Serrano; as well as by Juan Antonio Guerrero (another great expert in the Buchón). According to these experts, the reason why the engines (and other components of the aircraft) was that the Spanish Government never came to request or buy the Daimler Benz DB 605A engines. According to José Luis González Serrano, possibly in 1942 an agreement was reached with the German Air Ministry for the acquisition of the aircraft, but in one of the sections of the signed document it could read: "Having not determined the Spanish Air Ministry the engine to use in this aircraft and not having the Messerschmitt enterprise of the necessary time for the study of the matching of the engine (with the fuselage)or for the manufacturing of the tools of the aircraft, these works will be carried out in Spain." All that Germany was going to send to Spain was reported below.:

" a) the plans of the Me 109 Ga-2 with Daimler Benz engine. Immediate delivery (3 months).

b) the plans for the tooling. Immediate delivery (3 months).

c) a fuselage as a sample to study manufacturing. Immediate delivery (3 months). "

According to José Luis González Serrano in his superb work on the Spanish derivatives of Bf 109, the cost of this shipment was 150000 Marks.

To better understand the history of this amazing version about the engines, Carlos Pérez San Emeterio, and José Luis González Serrano tells us that the French designer Emil Dewoitine arrived in Spain when the Germans occupied France in 1940. Due to its great value in the aeronautical industry French, quickly in Spain ended up working in Spanish Hispano Suiza.

While the Spanish Government was trying to get combat aircraft (as well as tanks, light weapons, etc.) in Germany, in Spain the Spanish Hispano Suiza was working on a project led by Dewoitine which was called Hispano Suiza HS-50. It was a modern fighter with a maximum speed of 650 km/h armed with 3 20 mm cannons and 2 7.92 mm machine guns derived from D.520 (it was actually derived from one of its developments known as D.551) and for Emil Dewoitine it was called D.600.

Only a 1:1 scale wooden model of the new combat aircraft was built, which was very similar in shape to the sturdy D.520 that flew during WW2 in French aviation, in Vichy, in Italy and Bulgaria. Because the Spanish Hispano Suiza was the manufacturer, the engine that was thought to use for this fighter, was also manufactured by Hispano Suiza, HS12-Z89 with 1300 HP (this engine was the Spanish version of its French equivalent HS-12Y). There is no doubt that this fighter would have been an aircraft of Spanish manufacturing with good performance and that it could have been the main fighter of the Spanish Air Force, but the decision to acquire the German aircraft (which represented the culmination of the European aeronautical industry during the first years of the WW2) had already been taken because the decision to equip the fighter units with the Bf 109 was sure (despite this, in March 1943 the Air Ministry was asked to approve the manufacturing project of the HS-50, although this hiring was never done).

But while the HS-50 would remain only as a memory in the drawings of its designer, the engine that was going to use the plane, the HS12-Z89, it was of interest to the Spanish Government, so it was decided to make several tests with the engine to assess the possibility of being used by Spanish aircraft. The engine HS12-Z89 had four direct injection valves and was working in it, Markus Birkigt, a Swiss engineer co-founder of Hispano Suiza, who had arrived in Spain after the defeat of France in 1940 (the work for the manufacture of this engine began in French Hispano Suiza and finalized in Spain).

The Spanish Government made the decision to secure the future of the engine for the Spanish fighter by manufacturing it in Spain, since the DB engines and spare parts from Germany would always depend on the situation of Germany in the war (and Spain had problems to obtain spare parts from Germany for the Bf 109s B, D, and E after the beginning of World War II).

The planning of the trials with the HS12-Z89 engine, had several steps: test the engine with a single aircraft, test the flight performance of the engine on the aircraft and finally (in case of success) begin the installation of the new engine in the 25 airframes of Bf 109 G-2 that the Spanish Air Force would request from the German Reich (to subsequently manufacture under license 200 Bf 109 in Spain). But the lack of experience of the Barcelona factory responsible for manufacturing the engine achieved almost unacceptable results: too heavy, little power and with significant oil losses. Let's start with the beginning:

The Spanish Government never came to request or buy the Daimler-Benz DB 605A engines for the Bf 109 G-2 purchased from Germany. In the picture we see a Daimler Benz DB 605 engine. [Public Domain by Stahlkocher]

HA-1112K1L manufacturing chain in the Hispano Aviación factory in Sevilla. We can see the match between the nose and the HS 12Z-17 engines that were an improved version of the HS 12Z-89 engines. [Courtesy of Juan Arráez]

- Choice of the aircraft: to do the project it was decided to choose one of the Bf 109 E-1 that the Spanish Air Force already had since 1939 (this aircraft was weary and battered because the flying hours that had it since it arrived in Spain during the SCW). The chosen fighter was the one registered as 6-119 (belonging to the 23rd Fighter Regiment 25 Group based in Reus) and moved to the Prat de Llobregat aerodrome at the end of 1942. There work began to remove the Daimler Benz engine and replace it for the HS12-Z89 of 1300 HP. This work was carried out by the engineers of the Hispano Suiza, among which were the German R. Hermann and the Spaniards M. Cerdá and E. Viejo, who had to make some modifications in the plane to fit the new engine in the old aircraft (E. Viejo already had experience in this matter because during the Spanish Civil War he adapted different engines to aircraft for the Spanish Republic in the facilities in Alicante). Unlike the Daimler Benz 605, the new engine was designed to be installed in the upright position but the main problem was that it rotated in the opposite direction, so the performance of the aircraft while flying was worse. For this adaptation of the engine, it was necessary to slightly redesign the nose of the Bf 109 E-1. As a resemblance of the difficulties of engineers to achieve the matching between the engine and the aircraft, we must remember that there were no previous tests in wind tunnels, so the engineers did their best.

- After the success of the aircraft-engine matching, a test period of the airplane began to check the performance of the new fighter. To carry out the test flights, a pilot with great experience on the flight with the Bf 109 was chosen and he was a veteran of the Blue Squadrons that had just returned from the USSR: Lieutenant Lacour Maciá.

According to the work of José Luis González Serrano, the first flight with the Bf 109 E-1 with the new HS12-Z89 engine took place from the aerodrome of Reus (Tarragona) on April 19, 1943. Lieutenant Lacour Maciá had a total of 16 test flights with the Bf 109 E-1 with the new

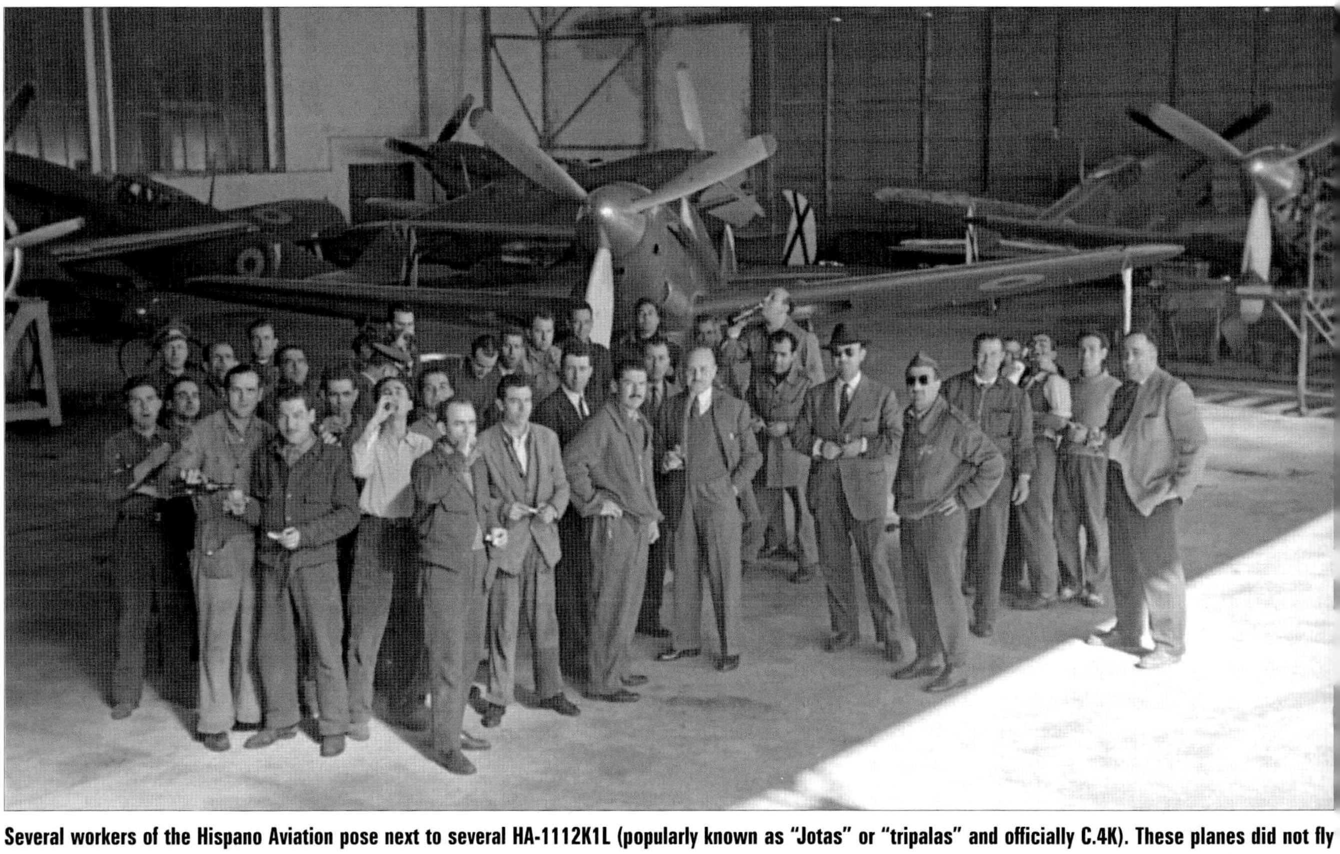

Several workers of the Hispano Aviation pose next to several HA-1112K1L (popularly known as "Jotas" or "tripalas" and officially C.4K). These planes did not fly until 1951 and entered service the following year, being removed from active service (which was very limited) between 1955 and 1956. [Courtesy of Juan Arráez by SHYCEA]

This Hispano HA-1109K1L of the 94 Flight Experimentation Squadron, as soon as it received its armament, it became HA-1112K1L in Torrejón de Ardoz. This three bladed HA-1112K1L (C.4J) looks like it was probably photographed in León in the mid-1950s and there it was used I several practices for the School until its definitive discharge. [Courtesy of Juan Arráez]

HS12-Z89 engine in Reus; being the last on May 20, 1943 (in total 5 hours and 44 minutes of flight). Subsequently, the trials in the fighter continued in the Flight Experimentation Group in Alcalá de Henares (Madrid).

During an intense period of time, the airplane and the pilot were subjected to various tests that resulted in an important success. In fact, the new aircraft achieved a higher speed than the original Bf 109 and excellent flight performances (horizontal speed, raise speed, and ceiling were similar or even superior to those obtained with the DB 601A) although problems of overheating were detected in the engine.

As a curiosity, José Luis González Serrano in his superb work about the Spanish Bf 109s relates that after the trials to which the Bf 109 E-1 was subjected with the new engine, the aircraft was dismantled the HS12-Z89 engine then it was re-engined with its own DB 601A. After this, the aircraft was returned to the 23rd Fighter Regiment.

- In short, the small problems that had arisen from the matching between aircraft and engine, were considered as very unimportant, so it was ordered the approval of the mounting of the new HS12-Z89 engines in the 25 Bf 109 G-2 that would be requested to Germany (and according to this version, this was the reason why when the 25 planes were requested, the corresponding engines were not requested). The nose of the aircraft was cleaned up with the oil coolers placed on either side of the lower forward fuselage in the middle half fairings and the carburetor air intake was moved rearwards between the main undercarriage legs.

Thanks to the works of the experts in the matter we can know with certainty that the Daimler Benz engines or the propellers never came to Spain because they were never requested from the German Government. Although it is also true that when finally Spain was able to start its program of re-engineering of the Bf 109 G-2, the WW2 was already completely decided in favor of the Allies so the arrival of spare parts, engines or other war arms would have been very uncertain and unlikely to perform (although it has been widely demonstrated that this was not the cause of the non-arrival in Spain of the Daimler Benz engines).

The Spanish Air Ministry was aware of the existence of the HS12-Z89 engine since 1940 and apparently after being accepted in the summer of 1943 to match it with the Bf 109 G-2 fuselage, the Spanish Government bought 50 engines from the Hispano Suiza in Barcelona. In fact, on July 22, 1943, the Air Ministry reached an agreement with Hispano Aviación for the acquisition of 200 HS12-Z89 engined Bf 109 Ga-2, for an amount of 70 million pesetas (approximately about 420000 euros). Thanks to the work of José Luis González Serrano, we can understand that in this agreement, the aircraft would be manufactured by Hipano Aviación "with its accessories, without engine, propellers, armament nor ammunition". All these elements should be supplied by the Air Ministry. La Hipano Aviación undertook to deliver the 200 aircraft in a maximum period of four years in the following way: 20 in 1944, 60 in 1945, 60 in 1946 and 60 in 1947, provided that the contract was signed before August 1, 1943 (fact that it did not happen) and that they received the original fuselage of the Bf 109 G from Germany. There were 25 fuselages of the Bf 109 G-2 that were purchased from Germany and it seems that they arrived in Spain in 1944.

The work was progressing slowly to match the HS12-Z89 engine in this case to the Bf 109 G-2s, in which Hispano Suiza engineers Hermann and Sardá and Hispano Aviación engineers Kindelán and Monet participated. These

The HA-1112K1L or C.4J (denomination of this aircraft in the Spanish Air Force) was popularly known as Tripala "(three bladed) only when its successor the four bladed HA-1112 M1L appeared. This survivor from the 65 HA-1112K1L manufactured is conserved in the Spanish Museum of Aeronautics and Astronautics was based during its career in Tablada, Morón, Torrejón de Ardoz and León between 1952 and 1955. It was delivered to the Air Museum in May 1971 and its preservation is superb. [By courtesy of Juan M González]

C.4J-10 (94-28) was saved from being scrapped by being sent to the Air Museum. When his picture was taken, it was still in a hangar at Cuatro Vientos airfield in the late 70s, before becoming one of the stars of the Air Museum. The HA-1112K1L (C.4J) were painted a medium bluish gray and their numbers in the fuselage were black. [Courtesy of Juan Arráez]

engineers took into account the poor performance of the VDM propeller in the Bf 109 E-1 with the HS12-Z89 engine, so they proposed the replacement of this propeller with another one, which finally was the Swiss Escher Wyss. Finally when after mounting the engine in 6 Bf 109 G-2s, we had to wait until March 2, 1945 (when World War II was completely decided and Germany almost defeated) so that the first prototype flew for the first time using a VDM prop (according to Guerrero it was a three-bladed Hamilton Standard) and lash-up engine mounting without cannon: the HA-1109 J1L was born (although at that time its name in Hispano Aviación was that of Me 109 J). The first number (1) corresponded to the number of aircraft engines and then these aircraft had the 109 included in their name since they were direct derivatives of Bf 109; although the official denomination that it received in the Spanish Air Force was C-12.

On the first flight of Me 109 J, the aircraft was piloted by Lieutenant Colonel Julio Salvador and lasted only 24 minutes (took off at 9.37 am and landed at 10.01 am). Later in 1945, the same pilot made 27 more flights (totaling 15 hours and 21 minutes).

The Spanish Government was determined to get the best of the HS12-Z89 engine, so from the first moments, it raised the study of two improved versions of the 12-ZA (with double speed and supercharging compressor) and the 12-ZB (with double speed compressor and intercooler).

After the initial flight, the first HA-1109 J1L was tested for two years, trying to delete the problems the aircraft had while flying. As we have said, between July 11 and October 17, 1945, 26 test flights were carried out by Lieutenant Colonel Julio Salvador (already with the Escher Wyss propeller on the aircraft); after these flights the aircraft was sent to INTA in Sevilla to continue the study of the new aircraft and try to improve the performance. The engine overheating that Lieutenant Lacour already observed with the test plane (based on the Bf 109 E-1), was tried to solve from the beginning with the installation of a large radiator in the lower part of the engine, but it was not definitely avoided. Other evident problems were the absence of basic instrumentation for the aircraft (such as barometer-altimeter recorder) or the excessive size of the air intake of the compressor or even the radiator too advanced position. At the beginning of 1946, after numerous test flights, the first Me 109 J was transferred to Alcalá de Henares (Madrid) to carry out the homologation flights of the aircraft with its new engine. There were 25 hours of flight and 50 tests on the ground with very disappointing results as we will tell you later.

The cost of each aircraft was very high so on July 23, 1946 it was decided to make a modification to the original contract between the Hispano Aviación and the Air Ministry, by which the Ministry would pay 110000000 pesetas for the 200 aircraft (from the total amount of money 8 million were used to pay for the first 25 aircraft and the different tools used by Hispano Aviación to manufacture the aircraft) and the Ministry also committed to provide the Hispano Aviación with basic instrumentation for the aircraft.

The remaining 24 aircraft (from the order that Spain had made to Germany) were manufactured during 1947-9 with Escher-Wyss propellers (also the first Me 109 J received its Escher-Wyss propeller after taking away the VDM with which it made its first flight). In August of 1947 15 Me 109 J were delivered (even without propeller or armament that had to be supplied by the Ministry) and between December 1947 and November 1948 aircraft had been delivered with serial numbers up to 40 (similar to the previous ones) aircraft, these did not have elements as basic as water and oil radiators or facilities for fuel. It was during 1948 when the aircraft denomination changed from Me 109 J to HA-1109 J1L.

The overall results with the new aircraft can be considered as unsatisfactory, which even motivated the Hispano Suiza to try to improve the

engine with the Turbomeca-Szydlowski-Planiol compressor instead of one of the Hispano Suiza itself (later we will discuss this evolution on the HS engine). The production of the first 50 engines was sent from Barcelona to Sevilla by road, but the manufacturer in Sevilla of the fuselages was carried out at a higher speed than the manufacture of the engines.

Of this first series of 25 aircraft called Hispano Aviación HA-1109 J1L (with military denomination of C.12, although later in January or February of 1951 the name was changed to C.4J), according to José Luis González Serrano, at least 6 aircraft received their engine (those of serial numbers 1, 2, 18, 81, 82 and 83) and possibly flew briefly with the Flight Experimentation Squadron, with the Fighter School of Morón and the 23rd Fighter Regiment of Reus; although they practically did not fly operationally due to the poor flight performance that was discovered once they were built. The performances of the old Spanish Bf 109 F (officially called C-10 in the Spanish Air Force and later C.4F) were superior to those shown by the HA-1109 J1L. On October 21, 1956, the Fighter School was disbanded, and the HA-1109 J1L that were deployed in it was retired.

After the many tests to which the first copy of the HA-1109 J1L was submitted in Alcalá de Henares, this aircraft returned to Sevilla where the tests continued. Finally, in July 1947, it was decided to suspend the homologation of the HS12-Z89 engine.

Due to the poor performance of the aircraft with the HS12-Z89 engine, it was thought again of its original engine, the Daimler Benz DB 605, to be assembled in the following aircraft that were manufactured in Spain, in the facilities of the Hispano Aviation in the Triana neighborhood (Sevilla). But the end of the WW2 with the German defeat and the blockade that the allied nations submitted to the Spanish regime led by Francisco Franco, would frustrate, as we will see, the acquisition of German engines for the Spanish planes (not only for the Bf 109 that were leaving to be manufactured in Spain under license, but also to the He 111 that would also be manufactured in Spain under license). On the other hand, obtaining new Hispano Suiza engines was considered necessary to continue with the project of an aircraft manufactured in Spain. All attempts of the Spanish Government to achieve adequate engines will be narrated in the following chapter.

Looking for engines

The Spanish Government, due to the international blockade, had great difficulties in purchasing engines for its Bf 109 and He 111 manufactured under license, for which it developed two ways to obtain them.

- The first way was the production under license in Spain of improved HS-12Z series engines (HS 12Z-17 engines); as well as the transformation of HS 12-Z89 engines into HS 12-Z-M that were similar to HS 12Z-17. The number of engines requested in 1947 to the Hispano-Suiza reached 150 and would be those used in the Bf 109 that were manufactured in Sevilla. These engines were manufactured in the facilities of the National Company of Autotrucks (Empresa Nacional de Autocamiones or ENASA) in San Andrés (Barcelona) and it was thought to manufacture them in the National Company of Aviation Engines S.A. (Empresa Nacional de Motores de Aviación S.A or ENAMASA). But the performance that the first HA-1109 J1L was showing with the HS motors, did not make it think that it was a perfect solution, so it started to work in a second way.

- The second way to get engines is situated in post-war Europe, in which huge amounts of war material were abandoned or stored by all European countries. Because the relations between the Spanish Government and other governments was unfeasible (motivated by the isolation of Spain after the WW2), Spanish agents began to probe the possibility of obtaining in the armament market in Europe, engines for the Bf 109 G and the He 111 H that were built in Spain under license. In this case, Spanish companies individu-

An HA-1112 K1L or C.4J in flight showing the 2 20 mm HS.404 cannons in the wings and the Oerlikon rockets under the wings. Although this aircraft had better performance than the HA-1109J1L, it did not perform well either. [By F. Andreu via Juan Arráez]

The first of the 2 two seat trainer HA-1110 K1L. The number of the aircraft is 199, and it can be seen painted with chalk on its vertical stabilizer. Subsequently it was changed its Hispano Suiza engine for a Rolls Royce Merlin, and was called HA-1112 M4L. [Courtesy of Juan Arráez]

Superb picture where we see a "tripala" with all its armament available in the Experimentation Flight Center (INTA) on July 9, 1956. The installation of the cannons on the wings and not on underwing gondolas was a very complicated job, and it was necessary to add fins on the sides of the cannons to prevent the flow of air could release it. [Courtesy of Juan Arráez]

ally requested war engines from other companies in Europe (in this way it seemed that the Spanish Government was not behind all this charade).

The Spanish aeronautical company C.A.S.A. (Construcciones Aeronáuticas Sociedad Anónima) searched incessantly in Europe for engines for the aircraft of German origin that it manufactured: the He 111 H. Because (unlike in the Spanish Bf 109) some Junkers Jumo engines had been received, the need it was not as huge as with the Daimler Benz engines for the fighters. The search was successful since in Poland they found these engines, which could not only be useful for the He 111 but could also be useful for the Bf 109 too (in the same way that in Czechoslovakia was carried out with the Avia S-199, although the results were quite mediocre).

During the Second World War, Messerschmitt Bf 109 aircraft were produced in factories in occupied Czechoslovakia. After the end of the war, production continued to be manufactured by the Avia Katowice aircraft with a DB 605 engine and Bf 109 G14 fuselage; aircraft with DB 605A engine and Bf 109 G12 fuselage (two crew) and aircraft with Junkers Jumo 211 F engine and Bf 109 G14 fuselage. The first ones were called S-99, the second CS-99 and the last S-199 (nicknamed "Mezek" or "Mule"). The combination of the airframe and the much heavier and more powerful powerplant was not ideal, resulting in a nose-heavy aircraft with poor handling characteristics.

In spite of being Poland under the control of the USSR and that Spain was considered internationally a fascist country, an agreement was reached so that the Junkers Jumo engines were sent from the harbor of Stettin to Stockholm where the Spanish engineers, in a semi-clandestine workshop, they would review the engines and embark on Sevilla what they considered suitable.

Simultaneously with the efforts made by the C.A.S.A., they contacted a British company that could supply (also unclearly) Rolls Royce engines, which could be used for Bf 109 Spaniards. La Hispano Aviación sent some of its engineers to the Hendon Aeronautic Festival to discreetly deal with the Rolls Royce enterprise.

Finally, it seemed that Spain would achieve with these two international efforts, obtaining engines for the He 111 (Junkers Jumo engines) and Bf 109 (the Rolls Royce engines). But in the postwar Europe with the western and the Soviet sides facing each other in what was called the Cold War, the secret services from both sides were very watchful to the trading movements that Spain was doing.

Finally, the Polish ambassador in the United Nations accused in the United Nations Security Council to Great Britain because they were trying to sell engines to Spain; so the British uncovered the "fraudulent trade with Junkers Jumo" that Poland had with Spain. Tension rose between the two blocks to finally solve everything by aborting both engines transfers to Spain. Because of this, the HS-12Z series of improved engines once again became the only Spanish alternative at that time to get aeronautical engines.

But in Europe, there were hundreds of aeronautical engines stored in various countries, so Spain continued to try to find some engines that were useful to their Bf 109 or He 111.

After an intense search and research of Spanish agents, a small number of Junkers Jumo engines were located in France stored since the end of the war. Without any proof of the material, it was bought immediately to prevent any political maneuver from ending up like previous attempts to buy engines in Poland and in Great Britain. To hide the purchase of the aeronautical engines, the Hispano Suiza factory in Barcelona (which after being nationalized in 1947 had been called the Empresa Nacional de Autocamiones or National Truck Company) was used as a cover, which "would use" those engines in buses. The purchase was a resounding success since the engines arrived in Spain, but as they had not been tested before buying, it turned out that since they had been stored in inadequate conditions of humidity, these engines were badly damaged. The Spanish anxiety to buy aeronautical engines had ended with resounding failure, in spite of which it was possible to put the Junkers Jumo engines in working order. But the distrust of those engines bought in France was so great, that the precaution was taken to mount in each He 111 (CASA 2111 in Spain) a Jumo from the French origin and one of the German originals that Spain had, so that at least the plane could land with this one if the French engine stopped.

Another photograph of C.4J-10 (94-28), this time assigned to the Flight Experimentation Center (INTA) where it arrived in 1955 and assigned those numerals. Shortly after it was sent to the Specialists School in León where it remained until 1971 and from there it was ceded to the Museum. [Courtesy of Juan Arráez]

Ha 1109 manufacturing continues

The manufacturing of the aircraft continued slowly, with the Hispano Aviación completing the aircraft with serial numbers 41-45, 47-65, 67-80 and 111-120 on June 30, 1950, 121-150 on December 6, 1950, and 151-200 on November 26, 1951. All these planes, as we have said, had no engine, propellers, armament, radiators, etc. A large number of aircraft manufactured without the possibility of being used motivated that they began to be stored in various warehouses in Sevilla, where they were waiting to receive their engines and other basic elements for the flight.

Spain wished eagerly to increase the number of fighters in the Spanish Air Force and could not wait to see if its attempts to obtain

The first film where the HA-1112 appeared as luxury "actors" was the German film "Der Stern von Afrika" (1957) or "The Star of Africa". This film was focused on the Luftwaffe ace, Hans-Joachim Marseille. In the photograph several HA-1112 K1Ls in Luftwaffe markings are scrambling; being able to see how difficult it is to differentiate Bf 109 F from HA-1112 K1L. [Courtesy of Juan Arráez]

Several HA-1112 K1Ls (C.4J) are lined up in Torrejón de Ardoz airbase in 1953 during the visit of a Minister. In this aircraft the armament was improved, so the HA-1112K1L had 2 20 mm Hispano-Suiza HS.404 or 408 cannon with 60 rounds each cannon in a fairing on the wings, then 8 80 mm Oerlikon rockets under the wings. [Courtesy of Juan Arráez]

aeronautical engines in Europe came to fruition clandestinely, so after the first 25 Me 109 J o HA-1109 J1L, it was decided continue with the serial production of the same Bf 109 G-2 but with a Hispano Suiza engine as well (this engine, unlike the Daimler-Benz, had the cylinders in V right and not inverted), although improved with respect to that of the HA-1109 J1L .

The engine chosen was the aforementioned Hispano Suiza HS 12Z-17 with Turbomeca-Szydlowski-Planiol compressor, very similar to the Hispano Suiza HS 12Z-89 that was manufactured in Spain (used in the HA-1109 J1L) but lighter, which allowed a better performance because it allowed more compression and less volume for a maximum power of 1300 HP, in addition to allowing a higher height compared to the HS 12Z-89 for the engine showed its maximum power (went from 4300 meters with the HS 12Z-89 at 6300 meters with the HS 12Z-89). In spite of the evident improvement, and the smaller losses of oil, the airplane was overheated enough with the small underwing radiators of the German airframes.

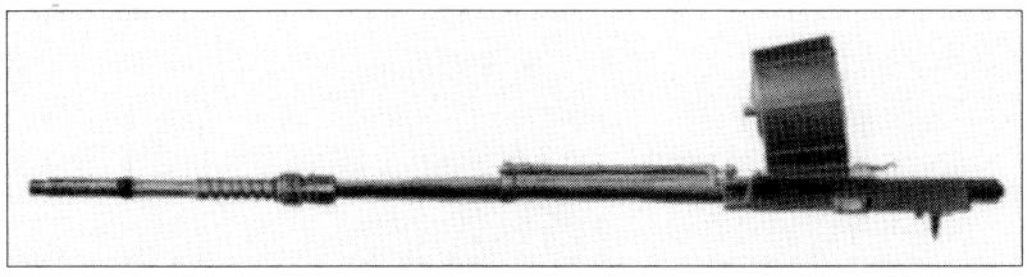

The 20 mm Hispano Suiza HS 404 cannon was the main armament chosen for the HA-1112M1L. Its fire rate was 780/rpm. The improved 20 mm Hispano Suiza HS 804 cannon was also used in the aircraft. [Public domain]

Picture of the Hispano Aviación factory in Seville (on 102 San Jacinto street in Triana neighborhood), where the HA-1112 was born. There, the aircraft were not manufactured, but they were also revised. We see the aircraft painted in cobalt blue and the "pelican" painted on the engine cowling, shortly thereafter were based in El Copero airbase. [Courtesy of Juan Arráez]

The HS 12Z-17 engines, as discussed above, began to be manufactured with French components in the facilities of the National Bus Company (ENASA) in Barcelona after an order of 280 engines by the Air Ministry at the beginning of 1948. Subsequently, at the beginning of 1950, another new agreement between ENASA and the Air Ministry allowed the transformation of 49 HS 12Z-89 engines into HS 12Z-17 engines. Really these claims of the Spanish Air Ministry were too high, since finally the 280 requested engines, became only 100 (which were also manufactured in France and later mounted in Spain) and the transformations of the 49 HS 12Z-89 engines in HS 12Z-17 engines, none was performed.

The 25 HA-1109 J1L were transferred in mid-August 1949 to the Tablada airfield, beginning the adaptation of the new engine to one of the fuselages in the next 70 aircraft batch. The date for the delivery of the new aircraft with HS 12Z-17 engines must have been between 1946 and 1947, but the slowness in the manufacture of the new engines and the delay in the signing of the contract for manufacture caused a significant delay. In fact, until April 1, 1955, only 45 HS 12Z-17 engines had been received and 100 were received in November 1956.

The new aircraft that was built in the Hispano Aviación in Sevilla already with the 12Z-17 engine received the denomination of HA-1109 K1L. Between April and October 1951 the HS 12Z-17 engine was installed in two prototypes; one with the British De Havilland PD/63/355/1 propeller and the other with the French Chauvière propeller, the winner being the first of the two propellers after comparing their performance. They were acquired 50 three bladed De Havilland PD/63/355/1 propellers and the license was acquired for its manufacture in Compañía Nacional de Hélices de Aviación S.A. or Aviation Propeller National Company (ENHASA). The name in Spain of this propeller built under license was HL 301.544. Evidently other changes were necessary to adapt the new engine, such as moving the radiator backward and adding two compressor air intakes (lateral and located at the bottom of the nose, to which slots were added to improve cooling).

The Air Ministry finally acquired 70 propellers (built under license in the company Earle from Bilbao). In January 1954 there were only two propellers manufactured in Spain, with seven more, almost finished. On April 1, 1955, nine had been delivered and it had to wait until January 31, 1957, for 45 to be delivered; being delivered the last propellers in 1959. As we will see later and very appropriately refers to José Luis González Serrano in his work, the last propellers manufactured in Spain under license were delivered when the aircraft that had to

On March 6, 1952, a contract was signed between the Spanish Air Ministry and Rolls Royce Ltd for the sale of 160 Merlin 500-29 engines for the Spanish He 111 (militarily denominated in Spain as B.2I) and 40 Merlin 500-45 for the HA-1112M1L (C.4K). In the picture we can see a Rolls Royce Merlin engine. [Public Domain by Jaw]

use them (the HA-1109 K1L), had already been obsolete and replaced in the production lines with another better performance model (the HA-1109 M1L).

The HA-1109K1L flew for the first time as a prototype in May 1951 with the test pilot of the Hispano Aviación, Juan Valiente at the controls (although according to José Luis González Serrano had to be another pilot possibly, since Juan Valiente did not receive the authorization to carry out test flights until December 1951). Only the first two copies of the aircraft received the name HA-1109 K1L, as it immediately changed to be called HA-1112 K1L at the time they received their weapons. This change in the denomination also meant that the 109 did not appear as in the HA-1109 J1L, and this was motivated because it was an aircraft that had been largely exceeded.

The new aircraft (HA-1112 K1L) had better performance than the HA-1109 J1L and some variants such as the redesign of the fuel tank (Spanish technology was not capable of manufacturing fuel tanks with rubber and self-sealing anti-projectile, so they were manufactured from aluminum).

As regards armament, the possibility of a cannon through the engine was immediately discarded and it was decided at the beginning the installation of two 12.7 mm Breda SAFAT (CETME) machine guns in an underwing gondola (due to the inability to install them in the upper part of the nose).

After some years of delay, finally in 1952 began the series production of the HA-1112 K1L. On July 15, 1952, a contract was signed between the Air Ministry and Hispano Aviación to acquire 100 single-seater aircraft HS 12Z-17 engined, but shortly after it was requested that 32 had to be two-seater aircraft, 18 as spare parts and 50 unmounted.

Finally, of the HA-1112 K1L, 65 copies (although a very much larger aircraft number was initially planned) were manufactured. Really only 40 were built (38 single-seaters and two

Beautiful photograph in which a solitary HA-1112 M1L without markings (except the Spanish badge and St. Andrew cross) waits at rest in an airstrip. This aircraft shows a greater height of the tail wheel, although this modification was not made in other aircraft. [Courtesy of Juan Arráe]

The HA-1112 M4L (C4K-112) was a conversion of the two-seat tandem trainer HA-1110 K1L in which a Rolls Royce Merlin engine and a four-bladed propeller was fitted to it. In this photograph we see it already in service with the 47 Group badge (based in Tablada airbase). In the Spanish Air Force, the two seat trainer was called C.4K, the same as the one seat fighter-bomber HA-1112 M1L. [Courtesy of Juan Arráez]

Photograph where we see one of the two HA-1112 M4L manufactured (two-seat trainer version of the HA-1112 M1L) damaged after an accident in 1963 that caused the aircraft to be discharged (C.4K-35). The other HA-1112 M4L (C4K-112) was discharged in 1965 while in flight condition and recovered in 1968 to film the movie "Battle of Britain". Nowadays fortunately this aircraft (C4K-112) still exists. [Courtesy of Juan Arráez]

two-seaters), to which we must add the 25 HA-1109 J1L that were updated and reconverted to HA-1112 K1L. According to José Luis González Serrano, there was an order of 35 HA-1109 K1L by the Air Ministry, of which only 20 became part of the Spanish Air Force for experimental use: flying in the 94 Flight Experimentation Squadron (Torrejón de Ardoz), with the Fighter School in Morón (Sevilla) and the 23rd Fighter Regiment in Reus (Tarragona). Of these 35 aircraft, on December 1, 1956, there was only one in flight (already with the name HA-1112 K1L), having been scrapped 3 and the remaining 31 aircraft were stored in the factories in Sevilla for further modification. In January 1959, 23 aircraft were still stored without the engine, for later cutting.

The engineers of the Hispano finally discarded the two machine guns and managed to install 2 20 mm cannons HS.404 cannons on the wings, as well as Oerlikon rocket launchers under the wings, so the aircraft was in its final version (initially as we have commented its armament consisted of one or two 12.7mm Breda machineguns and 80mm rockets eight-packs). The installation on the wings and not underwing gondolas was a very complicated job that the A. Figueroa team managed to finish successfully; it was necessary to add some fins on the sides of the cannons to prevent the flow of air could release it. These fins were maintained with or without armament since they improved the maneuverability of the aircraft, which ensured better piloting at high power. This was later revealed in the first jets.

With the new engine, they tried to solve various problems that the HA-1109 J1L had shown during its use. The HA-1112 K1L, which was later known as "Tripala" (Three bladed) by the pilots and ground crew, had in its final version a de Havilland Hydromatic propeller, 80 mm rockets and two 20 mm Hispano 404/804 cannons.

As we have said, since the beginning of its manufacture the Hispano Aviación engineers had to solve various problems, some as important as the engine HS 12Z-17 originally had a larger diameter propeller than adequate and had to import another smaller and less inertial torque (the latter due to which it turned upside down that DB 605). Other important changes in the new aircraft were the replacement of electrical cables made in Spain by other made in Germany (those of Spanish origin had been damaged by the effect of the sun), the anti-thermal switches (made in Spain were replaced by other Siemens made), the landing gear oil pumps (that had to be acquired in Germany) or the improvement in the joint of the wings with the fuselage (in the 25 HA-1109 J1Ls there had been cracks in the joints). With all these modifications, the number of aircraft that was manufactured in Sevilla was increasing, although the engines were not manufactured at the same speed. The aircraft waiting for their engines were stored in different places in Sevilla; according to Juan A. Guerrero in 1950 the aircraft with numbers 80 to 120 had been stored, in 1951 the aircraft numbers 121 to 170 were stored, to which another 50 aircraft were added in 1952.

Simultaneously we worked with new versions of HA-1109, such as HA-1109 M1L or in new variants such as HA-1110 K1L, HA-1109 K2L, HA-1109 K3L, HA-1110 M1L or HA-1111 K1L.

The HA-1109 M1L was a remodeled HA-1109 K1L with a Merlin engine. Of this model, only one copy was built.

The HA-1110 K1L was a two-seat trainer version with the Hispano Suiza 12Z-17 engine. It began working on this prototype in 1951 and was also called "tripala". Two copies were built. The first of the aircraft trainer took off in October 1953. These aircraft had neither armament nor central fuel tank (which was replaced by one under the second cockpit seat).

The HA-1110 M1L was a two-seat trainer version with the Merlin engine project; although it remained in the project since no copy was ever made.

The HA-1111 K1L was a two-seat trainer version with the Hispano Suiza engine and fuel tanks at the wing tips; that also remained in the project since no copy was ever made.

Picture of a HA-1112 M1L or C.4K in El Prat airport. We can see the two 20 mm Hispano Suiza cannons. The cannons have a total lenght of 2115 cm, 12 flutes at 7°, rate of fire 710-840 rpm with 120 round disintegration link belt; initial projectile speed 840 m/sg and a total weapon weight of 52 Kg. [Courtesy of Juan Arráez]

The C.4K-114 (471-39) still waiting for its wings in Rockcliffe Canada Aviation Museum. Since 1959, the possibility of changing the color of the painting of the Wing 7 Buchones began to be evaluated, and between 1962-1963 they went from having a cobalt blue color to having a finish in natural metal upper surfaces and light blue undersides. [Public domain by aeroprints.com]

Another experiment resulted in the single-seater HA-1109 K2L in which the two machine guns had been installed on the nose, completing their offensive power with the Oerlikon rockets under the wings. Another single-seater version was the HA-1109 K3L, which had no cannons or machine guns and was only armed with Oerlikon rockets. Both variants of the aircraft were finally discarded for serial manufacturing. At last, the winner was the HA-1109 K1L later known as HA-1112 K1L.

The military denomination of this aircraft (the HA-1112 K1L) was C.4J and as we commented previously they were delivered to the Spanish Air Force about 20 aircraft. These aircraft were distributed as follows: 14 were based at the Morón Fighter Academy (based in Sevilla), 1 was assigned to 23 Group (based in Reus) and 4-6 were assigned to the Flight Experimentation Center (INTA) based at Torrejón de Ardoz were they underwent extensive testing. The rest of the C.4J (with the two two-seat trainers) stayed at the San Pablo airport in Sevilla almost without use. The rest of the production, as we have told, was stored waiting to incorporate the engine in them.

The HA-1112 K1L was presented to a Portuguese commission interested in acquiring a close support aircraft, which finally did not come to fruition. The aircraft for Portugal would have been armed with Oerlikon rocket launchers and two 20 mm cannons, as it happened with the Spanish.

As we have said, the HA-1112 K1L did not fly until 1951 and entered service in 1952, being removed from operations between 1955-1956, when its replacement began to appear: the HA-1112 M1L. The last 15 12Z engines were delivered in November 1956, when the HA-1112 M1L had completely replaced the HA-1112 K1L in the production line. In fact, as an initial modification of the HA-1112 K1L Air Ministry's order, on September 27, 1954, 35 aircraft with Roll Royce Merlin engines were ordered, as well as two two-seat aircraft with HS 12Z-17 engine. The first of the two-seat aircraft made its first flight in October 1953 piloted by Captain Santa Cruz, and the following month the two-seat aircraft were already making test flights at the Sevilla airport.

Recall that in December 1953, the Spanish Air Force had only 32 fighters: 10 Cr.32, 6 Bf 109 B, E and F, 14 C.4J (in experimentation) and 2 Polikarpov I.15 Bis.

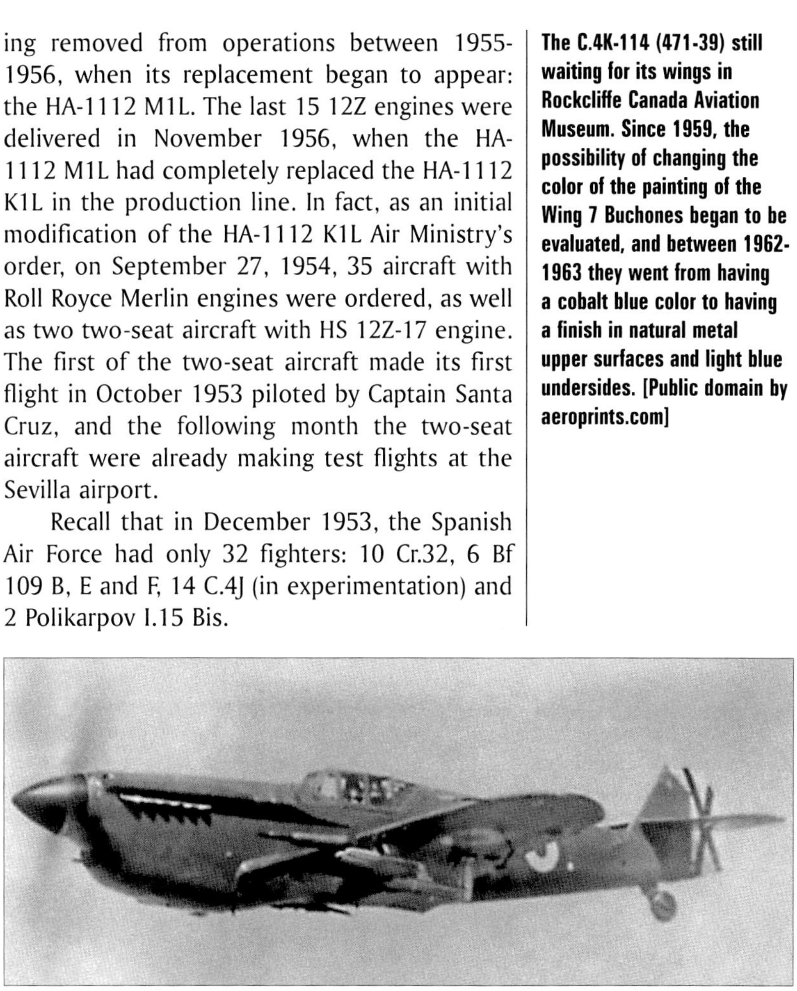

A HA-1112 M1L in flight showing its powerful armament: 8 Oerlikon rockets and 2 20 mm cannons. The HA-1112 M1L usually were not adequately equipped with radiocompass or with oxygen in the cockpit (the latter was not as important due to the use as fighter-bomber of the aircraft). [Courtesy of Juan Arráez]

Beautiful picture of a flight of several Wing 7 Buchones during a training flight. The last Bf 109 offspring were at least as elegant in the sky as their comrades made in Germany. The bulge of the radiocompass in the underside of the fuselage is appreciated. [Courtesy of Juan Arráez]

While the HA-1112 K1L was being born in Spain, thousands of kilometers away, in Korea the combats between American and Soviet jets were happening (the F-80, F-84, F-86, and MiG-15 were the chiefs in the Korean skies). This fact is a sample of the important technological gap of Spain in war armament (just over 10 years ago, in Spain flew the most modern aircraft in the world during the SCW) motivated by the isolation and international economic blockade that Spain was suffering.

As we have said before, the manufacture of the French engine in Barcelona with French components also began to be problematic since the stop of the manufacture of the engine in France together with the important deficiencies in the engines and the delays delivery, motivated the Spanish Government to think about alternative solutions to motorize their 109. Much of the challenges in the delivery of engines was motivated by the arrival of very few components and very slowly for the manufacture of the engine, apart from the high price that represented for ENASA the almost artisanal manufacture of the engines.

On July 29, 1949, C.A.S.A. signed a contract (possibly with the Society of British Aircraft Constructors) for the acquisition of two Merlin 500-29 engines, for installation in the He 111 that C.A.S.A. manufactured in Spain under German license. With these engines, it was tried to prove the suitability of that engine to replace the old and weary Junkers Jumo. Precisely in the early fifties, it was when the international economic blockade began to let finally producing the dropping of arms embargoes in 1952. Thanks to this new situation, the Spanish Government decided to give a new impetus to its aeronautical industry and began to work again in the search for a suitable engine to replace the Hispano Suiza engine of the HA-1112 K1L with another one with more features (it also happened with the need to replace the Junkers Jumo engines of the Spanish CASA 2111 with newer ones). The reason for the search for a new engine is twofold since obviously the arrival of new engines was an obvious desire of the Spanish Government, but on the other hand, the supply of Hispano Suiza engines was limited as we commented previously; so the search began immediately. The only possible alternative was the British Rolls Royce Merlin engine which was available. Really the negotiations began with the Rolls Royce from 1947 during the Hendon Air Show and were made by Ricardo Monet (worker of Hispano Aviaciónn), but it was not until the dropping of arms embargos in 1952 that those engines could be bought by Spain.

On March 6, 1952, a contract was signed between the Spanish Air Ministry and Rolls Royce Ltd for the sale of 160 Merlin 500-29 engines for the He 111 Spaniards (militarily denominated in Spain as B.2I) and 40 Merlin 500-45 for the HA-1112 M1L (C.4K). On March 19, 1952, a new contract was signed whereby the Rolls Royce supplied Spain with 160 Merlin 500-45 engines and 8 Merlin 500-29 engines. We can see that there were about two hundred Merlin 500-45 engines that were purchased to power the C.4K (although 32 engines were used as spare parts).

Meanwhile, in Spain, the aircraft continued to develop, and in October 1953 the first HA-1110 K1L (of the two that was manufactured) made its

A HA-1112M1L landed showing its armament:8 Oerlikon rockets and 2 20 mm cannons. Usually the HA-1112M1L had 8 Oerlikon HSS R-80 rockets attached to four Pilatus type MMM double launchers under the wings, with convergence between 400 and 500 m. [By F. Andreu via Juan Arráez]

C.4K-71 with numeral 7-52 belonging to Wing 7 based in El Copero (Sevilla) after suffering an accident. The history of C.4K was full of accidents. 123 HA-1112 M1Ls or C.4Ks were discharged after suffering an accident. [By F. Andreu via Juan Arráez]

first flight. As we will have the opportunity to know later, these two aircraft trainers returned to have a new life with a new engine soon after. The flights of the HA-1112 K1L after the arrival of the HA-1112 M1L had to stop in 1958.

The Buchón is born

The HA-1112 K1L manufacturing continued in the Hispano Aviación facilities in Sevilla (in San Jacinto Street 102 in the neighborhood of Triana), but engineers were already beginning to think about the incorporation of the new engine in the airframes from their Bf 109 G-2 (or HA-1112 K1L if it mounted the Hispano Suiza engine). As we have said, since 1952 the negotiations with Great Britain begin and quickly the acquisition by Spain of 200 Rolls Royce Merlin 500-45 engines is agreed together with 200 British made Rotol R.116/4 F5/11 four-bladed propellers (the engine was very good, although in Britain the main combat aircraft were jets, so at that time they were no longer useful). The first 155 propellers were already in Spain on October 17, 1956, along with 91 spinners; and it was not until January 31, 1957, that all the propellers and spinners bought were already in Spain.

This new 12 cylinders in line engine with 1,600 HP (1660 when taking off and 1130 HP at 5100 meters) was a single stage two-speed version based on those used for the De Havilland Mosquito and ironically had equipped the old enemy of Bf 109, the Spitfire; and now it would be the one that would allow flying to the German origin aircraft in this new stage of its life. This version of the Merlin engine had been designed for use in transport aircraft mainly. The combination of the ex-German airframe and British powerplant was successful. Interestingly, the first engine that used the Bf 109 (Bf 109 V1) was a Rolls Royce Kestrel, and now the last descendant of the Bf 109, it would also use another Rolls Royce engine.

The work in the Hispano Aviación facilities in Sevilla focused on the first moment in the adaptation of the new engines to the unengined HA-1112 K1L airframes, thanks to the scale model of the British engine that arrived in Sevilla at the end of 1953. Others Various modifications were made to the new aircraft, as the replacement of its three-bladed propeller by a British made Rotol four-bladed propeller. Given the important changes with respect to the aircraft model previously in production, the aircraft was called HA-1112 M1L; although unofficially due to the Rotol four-bladed propeller this series of aircraft was called "cuatripala" (four bladed) to differentiate them from the series HA-1112K1L popularly known as "Tripalas" or "Jotas" (because the J).

A flight of HA-1112 M1L or C.4Ks while training. These aircraft were deployed in El Copero airbase. [By F. Andreu via Juan Arráez]

Several HA-1112 M1L in a training flight. The numeral of these aircraft indicates that they belong to the 71 Fighter-bomber Tactical Squadron based in El Copero. [By F. Andreu via Juan Arráez]

Photograph taken in 1960 in El Copero airbase where we can appreciate the C.4K dubbed "PAQUI" and the 71 Fighter-bomber Tactical Squadron badge (a pelican over a white edged black 71). You can see voluminous Rolls-Royce Merlin engine and the four bladed propeller. The pilots of the 71 Fighter-bomber Tactical Squadron used to baptize the airplanes with the name of their friends, girlfriends or wives. [By F. Andreu via Juan Arráez]

On November 25, 1954, it was agreed between the Hispano Aviación and the Air Ministry, the adaptation of the Merlin engine in the HA-1112 K1L.

The Spanish made HA-1112M1Ls were not equipped with radiocompass or with oxygen in the cockpit. This picture shows the instrument panel and control column of a HA-1112 M1L, that its best was the great resistance of its armor, which saved many lives of pilots in the various accidents suffered by these aircraft. [Courtesy of Warbirds]

Several pilots of the 71 Fighter-bomber Tactical Squad next to an HA-1112 M1L in El Copero airbase in 1960. Behind them, we can see the 71 Tactical Squad of Fighter-bomber badge. [By F. Andreu via Juan Arráez]

Among the old types of aircraft that were sent to the Sidi Ifni war were the HA-1112M1L, the Ju 52 (C.A.S.A. 352), the C.A.S.A. 2111 or the T-6 Texan two-seater trainers, although at that time Spain already had the North American F-86 Sabre. In the photograph we can see a Spanish made C.A.S.A 2111 from the Spanish Air Force. [Public Domain by Curimedia photography]

It is important to remember that the redesign work on the airplane began when the Rolls Royce engine model arrived at the Hispano Aviación facilities in Sevilla. The designs were executed by the engineers Figueroa, Rubio and Ruz with great effort but with great success also given the difficulty of their mission. It was in 1954 when the Merlin engines were installed in two aircraft without the engine that was stored (the manufacturing of these aircraft had been completed on November 26, 1951). Without having performed any tests in an aerodynamic tunnel, the aircraft was completed finally on December 29, 1954, when the first HA-1112 M1L (fuselage number 197) piloted by Juan Valiente flew from San Pablo airport with its new engine. Much more powerful and showing important changes in its silhouette due to the presence of the new engine (it did not fit in the airframe inherited from the Bf 109 so it had to redesign the cowling to give it accommodation evidencing the differences in the Merlin engines air intakes compared with that of the Hispano Suiza or Daimler Benz engines) due to the bulky appearance of the engine's lower cowling, which gave it a thicker appearance than that of the previous Spanish fighters, similar to a craw Pigeon, for what was called unofficially by the workers of Hispano Aviación to this plane as "Buchón" or "Pouter" in English (the Daimler Benz engine, took the air laterally, on the one hand, the Hispano Suiza engine took it on both sides laterally, and the Rolls Royce Merlin 500-45 engine had its entrance to the carburetor and compressor; so the craw was to drive the air to the new lower intake of the British engine).

Interestingly the emblem that bore the Buchones (the plural for Buchón) in their noses was a diving pelican but not a Pouter. Long eyebrow shaped bulges in the upper engine cover similar in style to the Griffon-powered Spitfire were necessary to include the Merlin in the Bf 109 fuselage. It's interesting to remember that this aircraft was the only Bf 109 that was fitted with a four-bladed propeller.

Although it was evident the craw of the plane, what is not so clear is if that name in Spanish was given by its resemblance to a pigeon or a pelican; this last animal was painted in several HA-1112M1L or Buchones (plural of Buchón after the common high breasted local pigeon) as he was familiarly called by the workers of Hispano Aviación in Sevilla (although normally the pilots called them Messer). The explanation of the name Buchón already we have told it, but one of the pelicans comes possibly from that that animal makes low flights on the waters, just as they made the pilots of the HA-1112M1L over the marshes of the Guadalquivir river.

It's very important to remember that all the HA-1112 K1Ls or HA-1112 M1Ls were known in

Spain (especially by the pilots) as the "Messer" whether they were fitted with Hispano Switzerland or Rolls-Royce engines.

The first flight had a serious problem that would go along with the Buchón throughout its operational life, as the propeller of the Rolls-Royce Merlin 500-45 engines turned in the opposite direction to that of the Hispano Suiza HS.12-Z-89 what did the plane unstable. After the first flight, and until November 10, 1956, 102 more flights were carried out to get the aircraft ready. Thanks to the superb work of José Luis González Serrano we can know that in all these flights, the real time of flight was 44 hours and 2 minutes, being the longest flight of 59 minutes. A series of minor modifications had to be made on the original project to minimize aircraft instability.

Also, the second prototype of HA-1112 M1L (fuselage number 198) made numerous test flights (71), being its first flight on July 12, 1955. The total number of flight hours was 30 hours and 21 minutes.

Both prototypes of HA-1112 M1L performed on November 12, 1956, a flight lasting 1 hour and 12 minutes from Sevilla to Torrejón de Ardoz, to be evaluated by the Flight Experimentation Squadron.

Torrejón de Ardoz was where the HA-1112 M1L (fuselage number 197) was tested to approve the adaptation of the four blade propeller in the Merlín engine; while in the HA-1112 M1L (fuselage number 198) the possibility of different armaments for the aircraft was studied (at the beginning they thought of two 12.7 mm CETME machine guns, but finally the two 20 mm cannons and rockets were chosen). Finally, on August 3, 1957, both aircraft made a flight to Sevilla to join the 71 Fighter-bomber Tactical Squadron, where they received their final license plates of C.4K-7 and C.4K-8.

The adaptation that had to be made in the airframe of the HA-1112 M1L was also important to fit the armament, since they had to cut the wing stringer and make various adaptations by the Hispano Aviación team lead by the engineer Ángel Figueroa.

In 1959 the first two HA-1112 M1L together with two other C.4J with new engines, were used to make the tests of fire with the cannons in flight.

Due to the important advances in aeronautics since the end of WW2, the Buchón was completely outdated to be used as a fighter (technological evolution and the Cold War had imposed a new type of high-performance jet interceptor). Spain, still suffering the period of international embargo, had to self-supply its Air Force with this obsolete fighter, although in a short time it was decided that its main use should be the attack to land and in a short time had to be used in combat in African territories

A Spanish made Ju 52 (C.A.S.A.352) in Luftwaffe markings (without swastica) belonging to EADS (Airbus). [Public Domain by Kogo Gfdl]

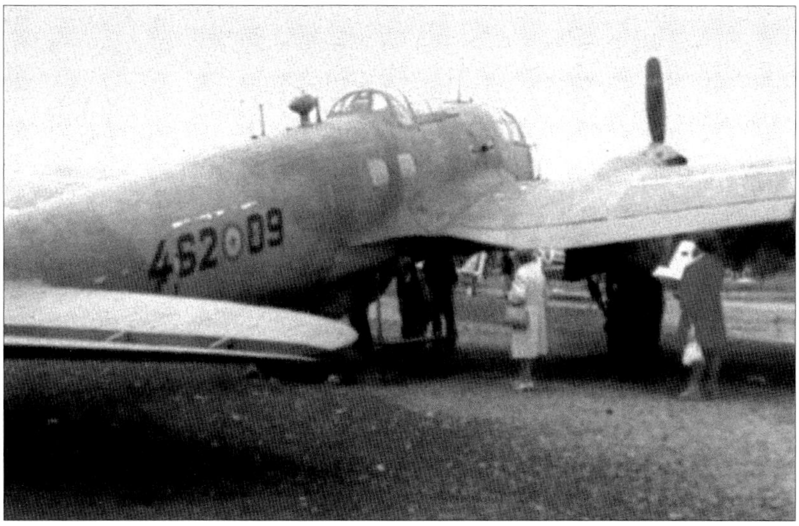

A Spanish made He 111 with Merlin 500-29 engines in 1975, denominated B.2I in the Spanish Air Force. Despite being an old aircraft, the proud bomber fulfilled its duty well during its war missions in the Sidi Ifni war. [Public Domain by Alexander Buschorn]

that Spain possessed. In one way or another, after the installation of the 404 or 804 cannons and the radio equipment STR and SCR-522, the military name of the Buchón was C.4K.

We must not forget that the new English engines were not only used in the Spanish Bf 109 G-2 airframes, but also served to fit a new engine in the Spanish CASA 2111 (He 111 H) that were also manufactured in Sevilla in the C.A.S.A. facilities.

With the cooperation agreements with the USA signed on September 24, 1953, modern aircraft consisting mainly of jets began to arrive in Spain. These agreements included:

- Help agreement for mutual defense.
- Financial assistance agreement.
- Defensive agreement.

At the beginning of 1954 the Spanish Air Force had about 900 aircraft, although only 600 were in flight conditions and were obsolete. The USA began to supply modern aircraft to Spain immediately, so in April 1954 the first T-33A jets and some sea rescue Grumman arrived. In 1955 the F-86F jet arrived at Getafe (Madrid), specifically on June 30, marking a milestone in the history of Spanish Aviation.

At last between 1955-1957, Spain received from USA about 200 F-86F "Sabre", 120 North American T-6D/G "Texan", 30 Locheed T-33A, 5 HU-16A Albatros, 15 Douglas C-47, and several helicopters.

Among the different types of aircraft that were sent to the Sidi Ifni war were the HA-1112M1L, the Ju 52, the C.A.S.A. 2111 and the two seat trainers T-6 Texan, even though at that time Spain already had the North American F-86 Sabre. In the picture we can see a restaured and flyable Texan in Spanish markings. [Public Domain by Marostegui]

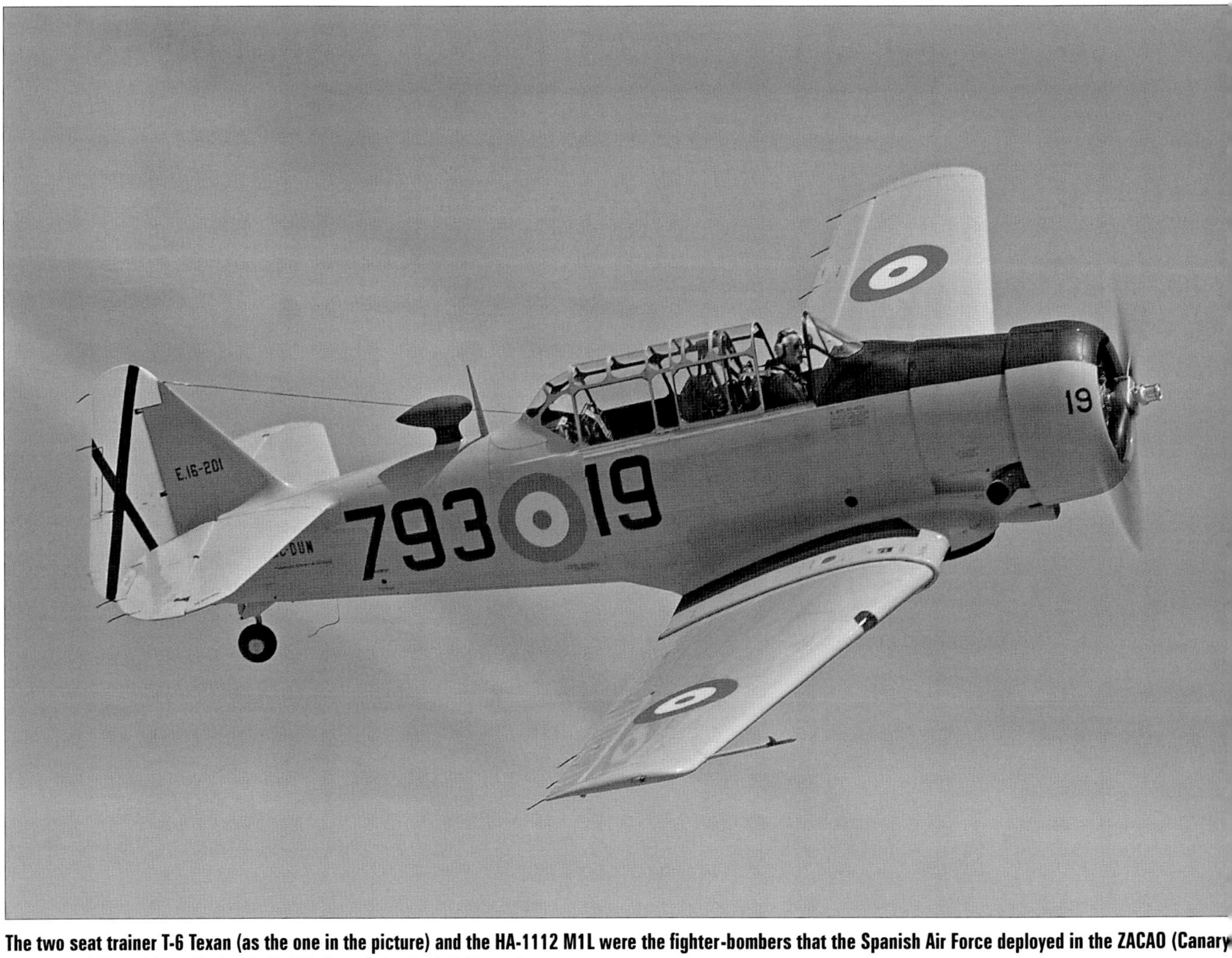

The two seat trainer T-6 Texan (as the one in the picture) and the HA-1112 M1L were the fighter-bombers that the Spanish Air Force deployed in the ZACAO (Canary Islands and West Africa Air Area). [Public Domain by José A Montes]

Before the arrival of these new and modern aircraft, the Spanish Air Force was undergoing numerous changes that made it an Air Force comparable to those of other European countries.

At the time, the Spanish aeronautical industry began to rise again (new aircraft were designed in Spain as the C-207 Azor or the HA-200 Saeta), but also, thanks to the agreements with the USA, the HA-1112 M1L it began to be suddenly completely obsolete for its role as a fighter within the Spanish Air Force.

Between 1954 and 1958, 172 HA-1112M1L were manufactured and delivered to 1960 and served between 1954 and 1965. Several of these HA-1112M1L were HA-1112K1L (possibly 35 aircraft) that were remotorized and upgraded to HA-1112M1L (the Air Ministry had to make changes to the initial contracts so that all the aircraft could finally have installed the Merlin engines).

In February of 1957 the HA-1112M1L state of affairs was: 2 prototypes in the Flight Experimentation Squadron (Torrejón de Ardoz), 10 in the airport of San Pablo (Sevilla) performing flight tests, 10 in advanced mounting phase, 20 in the assembly phase and 93 fuselages were overhauled (remember that many of the aircraft without engine were stored for years in some cases in the open air and therefore were not in perfect condition).

The entry into operational service of the Buchones was in 1957, when the first HA-1112 M1L (in theory they had to be 25 aircraft, but in fact the planes were arriving gently) were sent on February 16, 1957 to the newly created 71 Fighter -bomber Tactical Squadron based in El Copero (Sevilla); that was exclusively created to use these aircraft. The airbase of El Copero had an area of 366 hectares and was only 5 kilometers from Sevilla and 4 kilometers from the airbase of Tablada.

This new Unit which was under Lieutenant Colonel Isidoro Comas Altadill command was growing little by little. Initially it only had two HA-1112 M1L (with military numerals C.4K-7 and C.4K-8), and little by little they were increasing in number, until reaching a total of 60 HA-1112 M1Ls.

Several pilots were selected to pilot the Buchones from the 23rd Fighter Regiment based in Reus because they had previously piloted the Bf 109 E and Bf 109 F.

The fuselages without motor that had been stored in Sevilla were incorporating the new British engines and also in the HA-1112 K1Ls were replaced their engines HS 12Z-17 by the Merlin engines.

The first two HA-1112 M1Ls were taken disassembled in a trailer towed by a truck (dubbed "Andrea Doria") from the factory on San Jacinto Street to the airport of San Pablo (Sevilla) where they were tested day after day to revise the faults and problems that would be detected. Interestingly, one of the problems that was revised during the tests that the two HA-1112M1Ls underwent, was to replace their original painting (blue)for another blue painting, this time it was a cobalt blue but of better quality since the original one was detached when the airplane flew leaving to see the original yellowish varnish that was painted in the Hispano Aviation facilities in Triana.

We see C.4K with numeral 71-13 belonging to the 71 Fighter-bomber Tactical Squadron during one of their visits to the Tenerife island; in this picture at Los Rodeos airport in 1959. [By F. Andreu via Juan Arráez]

The C.4K-54 with numeral 36-406 in Gando airbase in 1959. This aircraft belonged first to the 71 Fighter-bomber Tactical Squadron then to the Mixed Wing 36, and was one of the aircraft that took off in September of 1953 from Sevilla towards Gando. The propeller is damaged. [By F. Andreu via Juan Arráez]

The C.4K with numeral 7-8 belonging to the Wing 7 in El Copero airbase in 1962. Since the creation of Wing 7, the digit 71 (because the 71 Fighter-bomber Tactical Squadron)ceased to be used. [By F. Andreu via Juan Arráez]

The color in which the Buchones were painted since they began their story in the Spanish Air Force at its base in El Copero, was the cobalt blue or Peugeot blue. In this photograph we see a HA-1112 M1L belonging to the 72 Fighter-bomber Tactical Squadron, because it shows its spinner painted yellow black split. [Courtesy of Warbirds]

The cobalt blue color, the "pelican" and the 71 or the 7 painted on the nose of the plane (the 71 was painted on the fuselage of the aircraft when the 71 Fighter-bomber Tactical Squadron was not subordinated to any other unit, while that the 7 was used by the aircraft when the Wing 7 was created), were the distinctive features of this unit born in Sevilla, although it also used other numbers corresponding to other units later.

The use of the pelican as a badge instead of the pigeon or pouter was possibly due to the similarity of the flights made by the HA-1112 M1L in low level fly and diving over the marshes of the Guadalquivir river, which recalled the behavior of these birds (other versions also cite the resemblance between the pelican and the profile of the plane). Recall that the name Buchón was created in the facilities of the Hispano Aviation, and pilots usually called the aircraft as "messers"

As it was already working with the new British engine, in 1954 the Spanish Air Force reduced the order of 100 HA-1112 K1Ls to only 37 and stopping at the same time the conversions by ENASA of the 12-Z-89 engines to 12-ZM engines so the last 15 engines were delivered in July 1956.

After the first two HA-1112 M1Ls (the two prototypes that came from the Flight Experimentation Squadron) that arrived at the newly created unit in Sevilla (71 Fighter-bomber Tactical Squadron) they did it on August 3, 1957, 3 more aircraft arrived immediately afterwards (C.4K-2, C.4K-3 and C.4K-4), four days after joining another aircraft (C.4K-5). In September, 6 more aircraft joined and at the end of December there were 23 HA-1112 M1L. As mentioned before, these aircraft formed the 71 Fighter-bomber Tactical Squadron before the Easter, 1957. Initially the airbase chosen for this Unit was Tablada (Sevilla), where was also deployed the C.A.S.A. 2111 (He 111 made in Spain) of the Spanish Air Force 25 Light Bomber Wing, although we will see how later this airbase was changed by El Copero airbase.

Although after the Civil War, Tablada was the most important aerodrome in southern Spain, but after the signing of cooperation agreements with the USA in 1953, it was no longer as important due to the lack of paved and wide airstrips.

The idea of sharing the aerodrome with the C.A.S.A. 2111, as well as other reasons, did not appeal to Comas, who thought that the perfect place for his new unit would be the El Copero aerodrome (as we discussed earlier, just four kilometers from Tablada).

Finally major Comas managed to convince their bosses about the suitability of El Copero against the airbase of Tablada, taking place on August 1, 1957 the change of airbase for the Buchones. El Copero airbase was practically in disuse from the SCW, had three hangars and provided the Buchón pilots a very large space with grass tracks, with the Guadalquivir River right next. The latter was the cause of important problems for the Buchones, since with the rainy season, it was frequent that the airbase was flooded and a lot of mud was formed as we will see throughout the operative life of the HA-1112 M1L.

At the beginning of the summer 1957 the Buchones moved to their new El Copero airbase

A flight of three HA-1112 M1L flying over Los Rodeos airport (Tenerife) in October 1959. We can see several landed aircraft: two Spanish made Junkers Ju 52 and one B.2I (Spanish made He 111). [By F. Andreu via Juan Arráez]

We can see the C.4K-9 with numeral 71-5 dubbed "MAPI" in the foreground and the C.4K with numeral 71-10 dubbed "CHIQUI" both belonging to the 71 Tactical Squadron of Fighter-bomber, in Tenerife in March 1959. [By F. Andreu via Juan Arráez]

(which had recently been abandoned by the Pilot Elementary School, which moved to Granada) and when the pilots' training with their new aircraft began (without having permission to take off with airplanes). At the beginning they were not allowed to fly but to do all the training on the ground. On August 1, 1957, all the Buchones of the 7th Fighter-bomber wing 71 Tactical Squadron had reached El Copero. The unit's number of aircraft was approximately 12 in the summer of 1957.

The trials with the airplane began and little by little the pilots were dominating the rough HA-1112M1L. At the military jets age, in El Copero, the pilots and the rest of the personnel belonging to the 7th Fighter-bomber wing 71 Tactical Squadron lived in an environment similar to that of the pilots in the first years of WW2. During this time, the pilots customized some of their aircraft with names like "Mapi", "Chiqui", "Checa", "El Teobal", "Pepi" (this aicraft was piloted by the brigade Palacín and also had a shark mouth painted on both sides of the air intake), "Loreto", "El Copero" (this aircraft belonged to major Comas), "El Sequeira", "La Cascajera", "El Mojama", "Inés", "El Trobal","El Toruño","Julía","Los Alcores" or "Con dos ...".

The training in the Buchones was planned to be carried out with the two-seater Buchón, but of the 60 planned trainer planes, the Hispano Aviación only made two (that initially had the HS12-Z17 engine and but until the end of 1957 those engines would not be replaced by the Rolls Royce Merlin and therefore came into operational service months later with the denomination HA-1112 M4L). This situation motivated that the pilots flew the HA-1112 M1L for the first time, completely on their own (as was done in times of the SCW in some moments) after a brief course to learn how to properly use all the instrumentation in the Buchón. The first flight with the HA-1112 M4L was made on October 10, 1957 by Pedro Santacruz. Recall that the HA-1112 M4L was the two-seat tandem HA-1110 K1L, but with the original engine replaced by the Rolls Royce.

From the beginning of the flights of the Buchón over El Copero, the pilots noticed the difficulties showed by the aircraft, since it was difficult to pilot and could stall without warning with the consequent danger for the pilot and his plane. In addition, the Buchón kept the inherited Bf 109 faults active as braking problems (every 6-7 landings it was obligatory to check the brakes since they were damaged) or those of the narrow and fragile under carriage.

The arrival of new HA-1112 M1L made the El Copero hangars not enough to shelter the aircraft. For this reason, many of the HA-1112 M1L had to stay abroad subjected to the weather conditions of intense cold and even more intense heat of Sevilla.

The situation in the Spanish African territories (Sahara and Sidi Ifni) was worsening so much that before the repeated attacks of Morocco at the end of 1957, Spain entered into an undeclared war to defend its possessions. Between the different types of airplanes that were sent to the combat were the HA-1112 M1L, the Ju 52, the C.A.S.A. 2111 or the tandem trainers T-6 Texan, although at that moment Spain already had the North American F-86 Sabre but the conditions imposed by the United States allowed that they could only be used on the Iberian Peninsula.

About the behavior of the Buchones destined in the Gando airbase and El Aaiún aerodrome to take part in the Ifni war that took place between 1957 and 1958, we will speak with more Depth about it in the following chapter.

Before Christmas 1957, the major Comas was ordered to prepare his unit to take off shortly to El Aaiún, for which it was necessary to use drop tanks. The only "small" problem was that the HA-1112 M1L did not have drop tanks, so it was necessary to design and build them in a record time, as we will discuss later in this text.

Nice photograph of one of the visits of the HA-1112 M1L from El Copero airbase, in Tenerife. We can appreciate the amplitude of the airport and the position down of the flaps. [By F. Andreu via Juan Arráez]

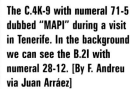

The C.4K-9 with numeral 71-5 dubbed "MAPI" during a visit in Tenerife. In the background we can see the B.2I with numeral 28-12. [By F. Andreu via Juan Arráez]

In this photograph we can see six HA-1112 M1L lined up in Tenerife during a visit to Tenerife. The elegance of the profile of these four bladed aircraft is evident. [By F. Andreu via Juan Arráez]

Sidi Ifni and Sahara

Thanks to the historian Carlos Pérez San Emeterio we know many details of the operative life of the HA-1112 M1L during the 50s and 60s and of course the history of Wing 7, where the HA-1112 M1L were deployed. An important part of the facts that we will narrate about the intervention of the Buchones in the Spanish West Africa and the Canary Islands (ZACAO or Zona Aérea de Canarias y África Occidental) will be based on their work, to which we will add information from other secondary sources.

After obtaining independence in 1956, Morocco began to express its interest in annexing Spanish possessions in Africa. The Moroccan sultan supported and financed the rebel bands of the Moroccan Liberation Army against Spanish territory. After the attacks from Morocco at the end of 1957 (on October 26 there was a hostile Moroccan act against a Spanish Ju 52 belonging to the 361st Squadron that was shot while carrying out a reconnaissance flight over Tafurdat) Spain entered into war with the North African country to defend their territories of Sidi Ifni the South Protectorate (Cape Juby and Villa Bens/Tarfaya) and Western Sahara. Apart from the Spanish Army and the Spanish Navy (Armada), the Spanish Air Force also took part in the conflict. The fighting that took place caused the Spanish troops 188 dead, 500 injured and about 40 missing in action.

In this photograph we can see the C.4K with numeral 71-11 dubbed "CHECA" and the 71-28 dubbed "LORETO". Along with the C.4K, there are two Texans (T-6D) in order to take part in the air festival that took place in October 1959. We can see the 71 Fighter-bomber Tactical Squadron badge in both aircraft. Both kind of aircraft took part in Sidi Ifni war. [Courtesy of Juan Arráez]

Another photograph of the "MAPI" (C.4K-9 with numeral 71-5) during one of his visits to the Los Rodeos airport (Tenerife) in February 1959. [By F. Andreu via Juan Arráez]

Bearing in mind that the Moroccan Air Force was practically non-existent and due to the demands of the USA not to use the modern American-made jets, it was resorted to the classic aircraft that the Spanish Air Force continued to use, such as the HA-1112M1L, the Ju 52 or C.A.S.A. 2111. The Buchón arrived just in time to take part in support missions and as a ground attack aircraft in the Ifni and Sahara conflicts being supported by the T-6 Texan two-seater trainers, suitably adapted to ground attack, from the French Armée de l'Air.

On November 14, 1957, the Spanish Army HQ staff met to decide on the measures that had to be adopted to solve the crisis in Sidi Ifni Among them was the increase number of Spanish combat aircraft in the Spanish West Africa they would be 24 C.A.S.A. 2111 (from Wing 25 based in Tablada, Wing 26 based in Los Llanos, Wing 27 based in Morón and Wing 28 based in Alcalá de Henares), 15-20 HA-1112 M1L and 15-20 North American Texan (T-6D).

As we commented previously, before the Christmas 1957 (December 20) it was ordered that as soon as possible, the HA-1112 M1L based on El Copero, take off towards Sidi Ifni and the Sahara. But these aircraft range was less than what they needed to reach their destination, and also the Buchones had no drop tanks so the only feasible possibility was to ship them to the Canary Islands and fly from there to Africa (although in the case of the Texans, the Spanish Air Force did allow their shipment on board). The Spanish Air Force did not consider the possibility of boarding their planes, so at the beginning of December 1957 major Comas Altadill (chief of the 71 Fighter-bomber Tactical Squadron) was informed that the HA-1112 M1L had to depart in a few days towards El Aaiún equipped with drop tanks. These absolutely handmade drop tanks should be designed, manufactured and tested immediately and the time given was only one day. This order was followed for three days of untiring work led by Jesús Salas Larrazabal in the Hispano Aviación facilities in the Triana neighborhood in Sevilla, which we will describe below.

During three days and nights, the team led by Sálas Larrazabal worked tirelessly to design and build the drop tank suitable for the Buchón After successfully achieving it and to verify that

A flight of HA-1112 M1L flying over the mouth of the Guadalquivir river in 1960. In this picture we can see that this C.4K (7-62) belonging to the Wing 7 does not have the cannons installed, although we can see the four Pilatus type MMM double launchers under the wings. [By F. Andreu via Juan Arráez]

Two HA-1112 M1L "resting" at the Malaga airport in the 1960's. Although both aircraft belong to the Wing 7 and were based in El Copero airbase, only the airplane in the foreground bears the 7 painted on the fuselage. [By José A. Rubio via J M. González]

the works had been carried out correctly, the Hispano Aviación pilot Fernando de Juan carried out the test by dropping the tank on El Copero with good results. Immediately several test flights were started with the new drop tank in the HA-1112 M1L, in this case carried out by the pilot Francisco Esteva, carrying out test flights with the same distance traveled, that the ones that the Buchones would have to carry out on their flight to Sidi Ifni.

The distance between Sevilla and El Aaiún was 1408 kilometers, which at a cruiser speed corresponded to a time of flight about 3 hours and 40 minutes. Bearing in mind that with the drop tank the autonomy of the aircraft reached up to 4 hours and 20 minutes, we can see that there was not much time for the brave Spanish pilots to successfully complete their transfer to Africa.

Meanwhile the period the pilots started to be chosen for the 71 Fighter-bomber Tactical Squadron Expeditionary Squadron (created at the beginning of 1957). There were 14 chosen pilots who must be added to major Comas in command of the small unit. From the 14 pilots, more than half were rookies with only about 300 flight hours (of which only 3 hours were piloting the Buchon) and came mostly from the Reus base.

The major Comas thought that it was necessary that the HA-1112 M1L had an inflatable raft under the seat of each pilotfor the dangerous and long journey to Sidi Ifni, but after several trials, it was considered impossible, so the idea was rejected. The pilots should arrive safely at their destination, knowing that if they fell into the sea, the fate was sealed.

Once the problem of the drop tanks was solved, the departure to Sidi Ifni had to be carried out immediately, but the HA-1112 M1L found themselves with another problem to start their journey, since due to the intense rains that turned their unpaved El Copero base into a mud field (the aircraft were sinking to the propeller), the planes with drop tanks with only the minimum fuel was considered necessary to facilitate their takeoff in the muddy El Copero on January 29 at Sevilla's civil airport (San Pablo airport), from where they finally started their flight to Africa.

Finally, on January 30, 1958, 15 Buchones took off from Sevilla under the command of the leader of the formation and leader of the 7 Wing, major Isidro Comas to Sidi Ifni. The 14 pilots that accompanied Comas were evidently pilots with little flight experience due to the haste with which the HA-1112 M1L had been requested in Africa.

The aircraft were completely armed (according to José Luis González Serrano, they did not carry ammunition for the cannons or rockets) and with the drop tanks that gave them the range to reach their destination (of the 15 planes, only 5 had radio and radio). These drop tanks were designed for a ferry flight between Sevilla and the Spanish territories in Africa and not to be used in combat missions. The flight was very long distance and having to exhaust the fuel of the newly designed drop tanks, they turned it into an authentic high-risk mission for the brave Spanish pilots.

In order to save as much fuel as possible, before the take off in Sevilla, the aircraft heated engines and then turned them off and refueled. After this, they were already authorized to take off.

Moments before taking off, the HA-1112 M1L dubbed as "Julia" and piloted by Captain Sanchez, had problems with the propeller, so he could not take off with his teammates. This fault kept him 4 more days in Sevilla and forced his pilot to have to make the solo flight to Sidi Ifni (which he would achieve with complete success).

The aircraft took off at two-minute intervals ahead of the HA-1112M1Ls flight, flying a T.3 (Douglas C-47) that continuously transmitted information about the weather conditions of the route between Sevilla and the Sidi Ifni aerodrome. The T.3 also transported four more pilots, several mechanics and varied material for the ground echelon.

For navigation, the pilots relied on radio beacons from Tangier, Larache, Rabat, Casablanca, Safi, Agadir, Sidi Ifni and El Aaiún. The

One HA-1112 M1L C.4K and a Texan lined up in Son San Juan airport. The HA-1112 M1L belonged to the 72 Fighter-bomber Tactical Squadron because the spinner is painted black and yellow. [Courtesy of Juan Arráez]

possibility of emergency landing at the nearest French aerodromes such as Port Lyautey, Casablanca or Agadir was also raised.

The pilots used the fuel from the drop tank in 6 transfers, the first two of 3 minutes, the two seconds of 4 minutes and the last two of 5 minutes. In this way, when filling the main tank with the fuel from the drop tank, the fuel was prevented from overflowing.

Once they landed the HA-1112 M1L in Sidi Ifni after 2 hours and 35 minutes. The airplanes arrived practically with the fuel tanks practically to zero, reason why they immediately refueled the airplane piloted by the commander and three more airplanes, that left hardly 15 minutes after landing, in the direction of El Aaiún (capital of the Western Sahara), arriving to the Western Sahara capital after 1 hour and 15 minutes of travel. The remaining HA-1112 M1L could not be refueled on January 30 at sunset, so they had to wait until the next day to take off for the capital of Western Sahara. Until that moment all the transfer of the HA-1112 M1L had gone without problems, but when the Spanish aircraft landed on January 31 in El Aaiún, the aircraft piloted by Lieutenant Barbadillo (C.4K-18), left the airstrip and clashed, leaving the plane with significant damage but fortunately the pilot was unharmed.

El Aaiún airfield had four airstrips made with gravel and compacted earth delimited with a small number of conical beacons for reference of the pilots. Outside the aerodrome, there were no natural obstacles to serve as a reference to the pilots, this situation together with the large dust clouds that the aircraft formed when maneuvered, caused emergency situations on numerous occasions. In fact, in many cases the pilots were more concerned with take offs and landings than with the fighting.

In total more than 100 combat aircraft (mostly outdated) were gathered in the area of Sidi Ifni, Canary Islands and Western Sahara on February 4, 1958: 30 B.2I (C.A.S.A. 2111), 30 T.2B (Ju 52) 12 E.16 (Texan) and 14 C.4K (HA-1112 M1L), in the main aircraft. That same day, the freighter "Río Jallas" arrived in the Canary Islands, where armaments were coming for Spanish troops, among which we can highlight 2224 Oérlikon rockets for Texan and HA-1112 M1L aircraft. Although the arrival of the Buchones in Africa motivated numerous improvisations in the Spanish Air Force, at least the supply of spare parts and armaments for the Spanish planes, of which they disposed in abundance, could be properly organized.

El Aaiún airfield was the main base of operations of Spanish aircraft sent to the conflict. The airstrip had good visibility but was very hard and had many stones (which decreased the grip of the wheels to the ground), which caused damage to some aircraft, especially in the HA-1112M1L.

The Sidi Ifni and Western Sahara conflict had begun about a month and a half earlier, so General Héctor Vázquez, Military Governor of the Sahara, did not give the pilots from Sevilla an adequate reception despite their risky and meritorious journey.

Once in Africa, the ground crew of the 71 Fighter-bomber Tactical Squad started working on the planes to have them ready for combat. In just two days, the HA-1112 M1L were ready to be used against the enemy despite the significant difficulties represented by the take off of the aircraft due to the immense dust clouds that were formed. There was not much to expect, since on February 2 they debuted with an armed recognition on Saquia El Hambra in which they can not see anything suspicious (the time of the flight was 1 hour and 23 minutes).

Both the Texan and the Buchones had entrusted armed reconnaissance and ground attack missions to support the Spanish Army troops. The Spanish pilots began with reconnaissance missions to familiarize themselves with the terrain. On February 3, the HA-1112 M1L received fire from enemy troops during their reconnaissance missions. The missions of search of enemy targets (rebellious bands belonging to the Moroccan Liberation Army) in the arid North African desert resulted in many unsuccessful occasions thanks to the rebels ease to hide in the desert, since most of theSpanish pilots that were seen were wild camels groups. Evidently the presence of the camels was very suspicious that not far away were enemy soldiers, but they managed to hide perfectly in the desert landscape. Due to this suspicion, the Spanish pilots received the order to fire on the camels with the 20mm guns, but it was forbidden the use of Oérlikon rockets because of their high cost (10,000 pesetas of that time, about 60 euros today).

The Bf 109 and therefore its descendant the HA-1112 M1L, were not especially well-prepared aircraft for ground reconnaissance, due to its high cruising speed and its tiny cockpit that allowed poor visibility. The pilots had to pass flush with the dunes under the intense desert sun, with great difficulty locating the enemies. Although in missions of armed reconnaissance, it was preferred the C.A.S.A. 2111, because of its slower flight and excellent visibility thanks to its fully glazed cockpit, both the HA-1112 M1Ls and the Texans were used in these tasks although with the ground attack as main mission.

Regarding the use of the Buchones cannons, it is necessary to comment on the emergency solution that the Spanish mechanics had to give to prevent the dust and sand of the desert from getting inside the cannons causing interruptions. The solution was simple and cheap, since condoms were used as a stopper in the mouths of weapons (that once in flight could be fired without any problem because they broke without problems). Several boxes of condoms were purchased in the Canary Islands (on Las Palmas island) and the Hispano Suiza guns problem disappeared immediately.

Between 3 and 6 February, the adverse weather conditions prevented flights of the HA-1112 M1L from being carried out. On February 7, 6 HA-1112 M1Ls carried out a reconnaissance mission on Lebtaina El Gueblía and Smara. That day, two HA-1112 M1L were damaged when taking off from El Aaiún airstrip due to the dust cloud that was formed while the aircraft took off.

On the 9th the HA-1112 M1L took off again to attack enemy settlements in Um El Fersig and Guleita Tafudart attacking the herds of lone camels with the 20mm explosive projectiles (120 20 mm rounds fired). The amount of dead camels was so important, that finally the stench they gave off when drying in the sun and the possibility of causing an infectious epidemic, determined that orders were received to stop shooting the camels if they did not see enemies with them.

But the main missions carried out by the HA-1112 M1L and its companion the North American T6 Texan consisted of the air protection to the troops and armament landings in El Aaiún beaches (in Western Sahara) during days 8 and 9 February. Thanks to the 20mm guns and the 80mm Oerlikon rockets, numerous rebel refuges located in mountains and caves were suitably harassed and destroyed. These flights at such low levels involved great risk not only for the characteristics of the terrain but for the exposure of Spanish aircraft to the fire of the Moroccan light weapons. Fortunately, none of the Buchones was shot down by enemy fire, but the poor conditions at their field aerodrome caused two casualties among the HA-1112 M1L. Due to the sandy airstrip every time the Buchones took off, a great cloud of sand rose that prevented the take off of a new plane until it did not spend several minutes. During that time, the pilot must have been waiting under a bright sun in his small cockpit, which sometimes motivated the pilots to try to take off before the sand was removed from the air. This precipitation resulted in two serious accidents in which the pilots did not suffer damage, but their aircraft were made scrap. We must also highlight the HA-1112 M1L inclination to fail the landing gear output, either one leg or both, which led to several violent landings.

On February 9 at the end of the day, only 12 HA-1112 M1L were ready to continue with the following combat missions.

On February 10, another HA-1112 M1L crashed when taking off (the C.4K-17), being out of service. After the return from the mission, another HA-1112 M1L (the C.4K-23) left the airstrip when landing. So, at the end of February 10, there were only 10 HA-1112 M1L left in suitable conditions to fly.

In the following days, the Texan and HA-1112 M1L continued to harass the enemies in Edchera, the Aureiegt Spur and close to the Lake Tennuaca; where the Spanish aircraft eliminated an important enemy resistance strong point thanks to the cannons and rockets. On February 11, the Buchones carried out an armed reconnaissance mission of one hour; on February 14 they flew over Uad Tigspert, Rem Abem-Itgui and Gor Um Echgaf for 1 hour and 20 minutes. The resolute and courageous actions of the Spanish pilots managed to make large enemy troop formations flee, avoiding ground combats, achieving that the Spanish Army columns achieved the aforementioned objectives. On the downside, the operatives HA-1112 M1Ls were reduced to 12 (due to the two lost aircraft, discussed above).

Picture of the C.4K-4 belonging to the 71 Fighter-bomber Tactical Squadron while it was deployed in the 64 Flight Experimentation Squadron (Torrejón de Ardoz) between May 1959 and March 1961. Its call sign was 64-4 (64 was the indicative of the Flight Experimentation Squadron, and 4 was the numeral of the aircraft). [Courtesy of Juan Arráez]

Several HA-1112 M1L lined up (where we highlight the famous "MAPI") in Los Rodeos airport in March 1959. Close to the Buchones, we can see a B.2I of the 291 Squadron (numeral 29-12). [Courtesy of Juan Arráez]

On February 13, after a reconnaissance and harassment flight over the enemy, an HA-1112 M1L had problems when landing (the C.4K-16 piloted by Captain Fernandez), leaving the plane out of service for the damages caused; so the number of HA-1112 M1L in good conditions to fly was only 9.

On February 16, the Buchones carried out their last war mission north of Gaada and Magder Tuama. Shortly after, it was considered that the Texans fulfilled the ground attack missions better than the Buchones, so it was decided to repatriate them. The same February 16 was given the order not to carry out more missions to the Buchones and to fly to the Gando airbase (considering the aircraft "unfit and bad"), when the number of operative HA-1112 M1Ls had been reduced to 9 only. That same day, another HA-1112 M1L suffered an accident when taking off leaving the aircraft destroyed although fortunately the pilot was unharmed (the C.4K-15), so that there were only 8 available HA-1112 M1L.

The HA-1112 M1L had done their duty in the little more than one hundred hours of flight they made, although evidently their original fighter mission was not the one they developed on the desert sands during the ground attacks (where their high speed and poor visibility from the cockpit they did not help at all). In addition to the small damages caused by the enemy light weapons, it is necessary to add the important wear of the airplanes in extreme temperature conditions that were from more than 45 at noon to below zero at night or with the great salinity of the environment due to the proximity of the sea, that corroded the Spanish planes fuselages. Many HA-1112 M1L had to be discharged by corrosion upon returning to mainland Spain.

Until then, the HA-1112 M1L had accumulated 102 hours and 41 minutes of flight, but the price had been very high, since almost half of the aircraft that took off from Sevilla were out of order. Although on February 17, another HA-1112 M1L that arrived from Sevilla joined the unit in El Aaiún (it made the flight accompanied by a T.3). According to José Luis González Serrano, this HA-1112 M1L was the one who had problems making the trip from Sevilla with his 14 companions, on January 30.

On February 25, the 9 HA-1112 M1L survivors flew from El Aaiún to the Gando airport (Canary Islands) in two phases. In the first phase, 7 HA-1112 M1L escorted by a B.2I flew on February 25; while in the second phase the remaining 3 HA-1112 M1L escorted by an AD.1 (a Grumman SA-16 seaplane) did the same on March 4. While they were in Gando, the aircraft carried out training flights every day, until March 28 when they moved to Sidi Ifni accompanied by a B.2I and an AD.1 (the flight from Gando took 1 hour and 35 minutes), finally on March 30 they take off towards Sevilla (to the El Copero airbase) escorted by a B.2I and a T.3 where they arrived without news after a time-flight of 3 hours and 34 minutes.

Some HA-1112 M1L were left in Gando and were sent progresively to Sevilla. Some did it flying while others had to do it by boat.

Making a general assessment of the HA-1112M1L behavior during its fighting time in Africa, the aircraft really resisted the difficult conditions in which they were used (extreme climates or very basic airstrips and with large amounts of stones and dust), being the accidents suffered mainly caused by the great difficulty represented by the take offs and landings from the airstrips together with the low visibility that the pilots had from the cockpit of the HA-1112 M1L. The HA-1112 M1L having a tail wheel and nose prevented the frontal visibility of the pilot, creating great difficulties to maneuver in airstrips with few beacons and with sand and stones like those of Sidi Ifni or El Aaiún.

Officially the Ifni/Sahara war ended in May 1958, but in reality the attacks on Spanish places and shootings against Spaniards continued during the following years causing several deaths and injuries, but the tension between Morocco and Spain would increase again soon. On April 1, the Angra de Cintra agreement was signed between Spain and Morocco, for which Spain delivered to Morocco Cabo Juby.

Since his return to the El Copero airbase, Major Comas began to solve some of the problems they had had when their planes were sent to Sidi Ifni. Above all, he managed to start the asphalting works of the airbase parking area (although the grass track continued to be used) to have a firm track in case of heavy rains that flooded the grass track.

The pilots who had flown the HA-1112 M1L towards Sidi Ifni had shown their bravery, but the need to improve the training was evidenced. Nine of the pilots sent to Africa did not arrive at 20 flight hours flying the HA-1112 M1L, and some of them had serious difficulties in basic maneuvers as take off and landing. For this, despite only having two tandem Buchones, their use increased a lot.

Return to the action of the Wing 7 Buchones

Although the tension in the Western Africa Spanish territories had calmed down, in the summer of 1958, the Spanish Air Force HQ decided that it was necessary to send a HA-1112M1Ls flight to deploy them in Gando's airbase. This small Unit was an extension of the 71 Fighter-bomber Tactical Squadron based in El Copero, to which they continued to belong.

Spain needed to control their territories in Western Africa, so on September 13, 1958, the new HA-1112M1L expedition took off from El Copero to Gando. 9 HA-1112M1Ls were sent together with a B.2I to Sidi Ifni and later to Gando where a 71 Fighter-bomber Tactical Squadron based detachment from El Copero was created and based in that Canarian aerodrome. The flight lasted 3 hours and 45 minutes to Sidi Ifni, and 1 hour and 45 minutesfrom Sidi Ifni to Gando. The arrival to Gando was on September 14 and from that time the HA-1112M1Ls carried out many armed reconnaissance missions watching the Western Africa Spanish territories demonstrating that the pilots skill improved day after day.

Fortunately, no new armed confrontations against the rebels required the use of Spanish combat aircraft, so no combat action was taken. Yes, there were numerous armed reconnaissance missions and real fire training. During the time that the HA-1112M1L (in their second visit to ZACAO) were based in Gando, only one aircraft was damaged due to a fire while it was landed.

In 1959, the number of HA-1112M1Ls was increasing, so in spring there were more than 100 aircraft. The large number of Buchones available in El Copero allowed a second combat unit to be created on March 2, 1959: the 72 Fighter-bomber Tactical Squadron. To shelter the two squadrons (71 and 72), an upper unit called 7 Fighter-bomber Wing (known as Wing 7) was also created. The 71 Fighter-bomber Tactical Squadron leader continued to be Commander Comas, the 72 Fighter-bomber Tactical Squadron leader was Commander Fernández and the Wing 7 leader was Lieutenent Colonel Fernández de Quincoces.

To differentiate the HA-1112M1Ls from the 71 Fighter-bomber Tactical Squadron belonging to the 72 Fighter-bomber Tactical Squadron, the 71 Squadron spinners were painted in red and the 72 Squadron spinners in yellow. This matter will be commented deeper in the chapter of Buchón´s camouflage.

Meanwhile, the small 71 Fighter-bomber Tactical Squadron detachment deployed in Gando, continued with its reconnaissance missions while improving its performance after continuous real fire practices. Finally the stay of the HA-1112M1Ls in Gando ended on April 26, 1960 when the aircraft returned to Sevilla.

During 1960, the Wing 7 had a quiet time with only a few Buchones outdated and scrapped. A curiosity that José Luis González

Beautiful photograph of the C.4K "MAPI" of the 71 Fighter-bomber Tactical Squadron during a visit to Palma de Mallorca (Son San Juan airport) in May 1964. After the C.4K-9 with numeral 71-5 it can be seen another unidentified aircraft. "MAPI" was one of the C.4K that took part in the first detachment to the Spanish Western Africa and the Canary Islands (ZACAO or Canary Islands Air Area and Spanish West Africa) on January 30, 1958. [Courtesy of Juan Arráez]

A flight of Ha-1112 M1L belonging to Mixed Wing 36 flying over the Canary Islands in 1959. The photo is a copy of the file from the Photography and Cartography Section in the Gando Base. [By F. Andreu via Juan Arráez]

Serrano refers to in his work is that for almost two years (from the creation of Wing 7 until December 1960), the HQ Squadron had more aircraft (71 HA-1112M1L) than each of its two Squadrons (25 HA-1112M1L the 71 Fighter-bomber Tactical Squadron and 25 HA-1112M1L the 72 Fighter-bomber Tactical Squadron).

But in 1961 the Spanish information services detected an imminent attack in Ifni and Sahara, rebel bands of the Moroccan Liberation Army, with the permission of Hassan II, the king of Morocco who began his reign in 1961. Among the measures adopted by the Spanish Government, it was ordered that the Spanish Air Force fighters and bombers had to be in alert status.

Again, and copying what was done during the 1957 conflict, for the third time the HA-1112M1Ls were sent to Africa to reinforce the Spanish military units; although this time their call to action fortunately did not take part in combat. On this occasion, along with the Wing 7, the Wing 3 Texans were also sent to Africa.

On March 21, 1961 (March 25 according to José Luis González Serrano), from the El Copero air base, 15 HA-1112M1Ls (12 according to José Luis González Serrano), took off in heading towards the main airport in Sevilla (San Pablo, again due to the heavy rains that had left the El Copero airbase waterlogged and therefore preventing them from taking off from there with all the weapons and drop tanks. There they made the last preparations in the Buchones so that they were ready for their flight towards Sidi Ifni. Already at the Sevilla airport, the Buchones were equipped with drop tanks. On March 25, finally the 15 HA-1112M1L took off towards Sidi Ifni, although one of the aircraft (the one piloted by the Madroño brigade) had to make an emergency landing next to Sevilla shortly after taking off.

The route of the HA-1112M1L went from Sevilla towards the Strait of Gibraltar, when the aircraft piloted by Lieutenant Lombarte had problems so he had to return to his base in El Copero.

Later the Buchón piloted by the Lieutenant Ruíz Nicolau (C4K 7-131) after about three hours of flight, he noticed a problem in the fuel gauge, which initially did not seem important but at last forced the pilot to make an emergency landing. Lieutenant Ruíz Nicolau landed on the beach of Aglu, 16 kilometers from Tifnit in Morocco and 60 kilometers or 10 minutes away from Sidi Ifni (prior to landing, he was ordered to shoot the rockets and empty the cannons, the first could be done by throwing them against the sea, but the cannons were jammed and it was not possible). Before landing on the beach, the pilot considered the possibility of landing next to a ship, but suspecting that it was Soviet, the Spanish pilot preferred to do it on the Moroccan beach. The pilot was trapped inside the cockpit as the tide rose, with the risk of drowning the Spanish driver. After about 3 hours trapped in his plane, Lieutenant Ruíz Nicolau was rescued by natives that were witness of the emergency landing and handed over the Spanish pilot to the Royal Moroccan Forces as a prisoner. After some difficult negotiations, finally the brave Spanish pilot was repatriated to Spain, specifically returned to the Wing 7 in El Copero (Sevilla).

The other HA-1112M1Ls of the expedition managed to reach Sidi Ifni after 3 hours and 20 minutes from Sevilla and later went to Gando, where they had to land in a narrow service airstrip, since the main airstip was under repair. After the incidents during the long flight, the Buchones did not have to take part against the Moroccan troops on this occasion, they only flew armed reconnaissance tasks over the desert. Due to the fact that fortunately the moment of highest tension between Morocco and Spain passed, the HA-1112M1L belonging to the Wing 7 returned to its base in El Copero.

After the return to the Iberian Peninsula, the HA-1112M1Ls were being removed slowly from active service in the Spanish Air Force. During this period, the pilots were able to show the high skill they had achieved after several years using the temperamental Buchones.

A demonstration of the capabilities of the Buchón took place during an air festival that took place at the Tablada aerodrome in May. During various acrobatic exercises, the Wing 7 pilots showed their skills in front of the Spanish head of the state Francisco Franco. Also during an air to ground simulation the Spanish pilots achieved 100% hits in their targets.

During 1961, the HA-1112M1Ls were being progressively withdrawn from the Spanish Air Force, being discharged 18 more aircraft.

The Buchones did a last flight towards Africa on July 31, 1962. There were 12 HA-1112M1Ls (8 according to José Luis González Serrano) to replace the numerous casualties suffered by the 72 Fighter-bomber Tactical Squadron deployed in Gando. The damaged aircraft returned to Sevilla by boat due they could not fly. The new HA-1112M1Ls took off that day towards Sidi Ifni where they arrived after a flight that lasted 3 hours and 15 minutes, from there the aircraft flew towards Gando. The number of HA-1112M1L in Gando was 18, all belonging to the 72 Fighter-bomber Tactical Squadron, although shortly after (in October 1962) they would also change units, being transferred to the 364 Squadron belonging to the new borned Mixed Wing 36.

In October of 1962, once the critical situation was solved, the Spanish Air Force expeditionary units were based at the Gando airport (Canary Islands) under the name Mixed Wing 36, which had the following squadrons:

- 361 Squadron: with Ju 52 (T.2B).
- 362 Squadron: with C.A.S.A. 2111 (B.2I).
- 363 Squadron: with Texan (E.16).
- 364 Squadron: with HA-1112M1L (there were 20 HA-1112M1L deployed in this Squadron).

In January of 1963 the 364 Squadron leader was Commander Timón. During the operational period of this squadron, numerous flight trainings, acrobatics and armed reconnaissance were carried out. Also in February 1963, 10 or 11 pilots were deployed in Villa Cisneros, whose airstrip was very basic and compacted earth. A few times, the pilots were deployed in El Aaiún. The 364 Squadron was disbanded possibly in August 1964, after two years and 805 flight hours since it was created.

After the Sidi Ifni and Sahara conflicts, the rest of the operational life of the Buchón was very quiet. From March 1963, Tablada was once again the Airbase for the last flights of the Buchones with Spanish Air Force badges on its

The C.4K with numeral 7-62 of the Wing 7 flying over the mouth of the Guadalquivir river in 1960. We can see the 71 Fighter-bomber Tactical Squadron badge (a pelican over a black 71). [By F. Andreu via Juan Arráez]

wings and fuselage (the frequent floods that occurred in El Copero airbase were largely cause of this transfer). On August 21, 1963, Colonel Simón began to be the Wing 7leader; he had pride in being the last leader of this unit.

Each year, more HA-1112M1Ls were withdrawn and flights became more scarce. In 1964, 44 HA-1112M1Ls were withdrawn and in 1965 all other Buchones still in service were discharged. Before being definitively put out of commission and discharged in October 1965, the Buchón had time to live together during this last year alongside the Spanish Air Force F-104G Starfighters (which arrived in January 1965 and were deployed in the 161 Squadron based in Torrejón de Ardoz).

Before the disappearance of the HA-1112M1L, in May 1965, the Wing 7 was renamed Wing 47, being the 471 Squadron its subordinate unit. This new Wing was commanded by Colonel Rafael Simón and was only in operational status for 4 months. The aircraft deployed in the 471 Squadron were the last Buchones that flew belonging to the Spanish Air Force.

The last flight of a Buchón in the Wing 47 took place on October 5, 1965 from the Tablada airfield. Curiously, it was the same aerodrome witness of the beginning and end of the history of Bf 109 in Spain. It was almost 30 years that passed since the Luftwaffe pilot Hans Trauloft landed in Tablada in November 1936 until the last flight of the HA-1112M1L took place. It was on November 19, 1965 when the Wing 47 was disbanded, ending the history of Bf 109 derivatives in the Spanish Air Force.

The most important Bf 109 derivate aircraft was without any doubt the HA-1112M1L, but its bad performance in the jet age, motivated that it was the Spanish fighter (although its use was really fighter-bomber) with less operational use in the Spanish Air Force. With 172 aircraft manufactured, for 9 years they did not reach 25000 flight hours. One of the causes that can explain their limited operational use was the large number of accidents suffered by these aircraft (123 were discharged after suffering an accident) due to how difficult it was to pilot it especially in the take offs and landings (where its narrow landing gear was a continuous source of problems) and of course to the inability to train the new pilots in the two-seat trainer HA-1112M4L since they were only manufactured 2. If the pilots had had an adequate training period, with two-seat trainers and would not have been sent to the war practically so soon, it is sure that the aircraft performance would have been better because they would had been piloted by pilots not only brave but also properly trained.

With the Buchones withdrawal, Tablada ran out of flight units and started the partial dismantling of its facilities. It seemed that the role of the Buchón in the History of Aviation had ended, but it was only its end in the Spanish Air Force since the aircraft of the Wing 47 were dismantled and stored to be scrapped later. But the miracle happened only two years later, when a company called "Spitfire Productions" went to the Spanish Air Force to buy the last Wing 47 18 Buchones that had not been scrapped in order to film a movie entitled "Battle of Britain". This fact allowed some of the Buchones managed to escape their destiny in the scrapyard and that thanks to the interest of various companies and people, can even today be flyables thanks to his role as an actor in films about WW2 and air festivals. But this story will be told in the section "The actor Buchón".

A star has born: the actor Buchón

The last Buchones retired from active duty in 1965, but undoubtedly for what is known the HA-1112 worldwide is for having become for many years the most used aircraft in war films to replace with credibility the German Bf 109s. After all, the HA-1112s are direct descendants of the German fighter, and sometimes without modifications and others with different arrangements to look more like Bf 109, have been used in several well-known films; among which we must highlight the wonderful "Battle of Britain" (1969).

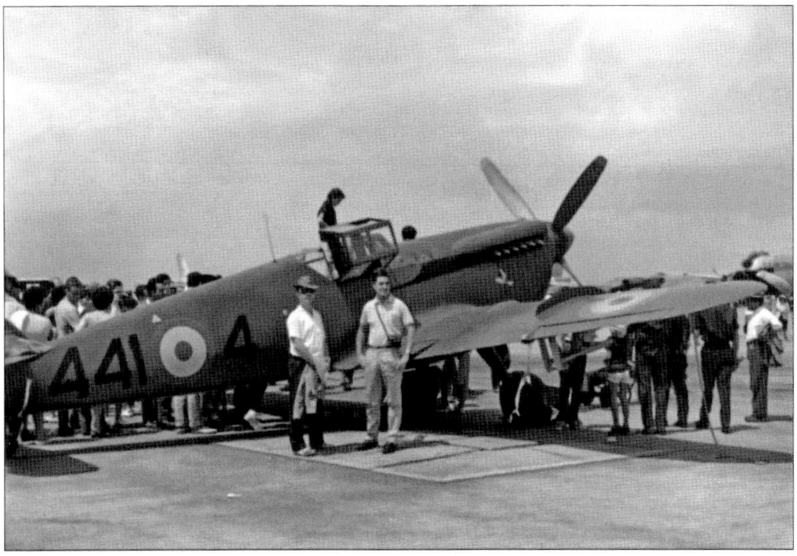

Pictured taken in 1962 in Torrejón de Ardoz airbase during an Air Festival. According to Juan M González this HA-1112 M1L (441-4) belonged to the 441 Experimental Flight Group Squadron at INTA. To the right we can see a C-124 Globemaster II. [By courtesy of Juan M González]

Thanks to the interest of keeping the HA-1112 able to fly, there have been many Spanish-made aircraft that have continued to fly not only in films, but in several air shows. In addition, there is still a high number of HA-1112s that are exposed in various museums both in its original model HA-1112 and converted into Bf 109. Currently a large part of the Bf 109 in flight or in museums are actually HA-1112K1L.

The first film where the HA-1112 appeared as luxury "actors", was the German film "Der Stern von Afrika" (1957) or "The Star of Africa" or "La estrella de África" in Spain. This film was a co-production between the German Neue Emelca and the Spanish Ariel Film and was focused on the Luftwaffe ace, Hans-Joachim Marseille. The aircraft model used for the film was the C.4J (Hispano Suiza engined), so the resemblance to the Bf 109 E and especially to the F model, was so great that it is difficult to differentiate both aircraft. In some cases the aircraft did not have weapons yet.

Filming took place mainly in Maspalomas (Gran Canaria) and the aircraft were transferred by boat to the Gando aerodrome, from where they could fly. Other scenes of the movie were filmed in Sevilla (Tablada and Morón de la Frontera). The C.4J made a lot of take offs and landings, as well as various taxiing scenes in the airstrip. The aerial combats were filmed with models and not with the C.4J.

But the film that definitely gave HA-1112M1L world fame and the one that revealed the potential of the Spanish Buchón in the movies was the "Battle of Britain" or "La Batalla de Inglaterra" in Spain, a legendary British film from 1969.

Because of its grandiosity and use of many flyables and static aircraft, the "Battle of Britain" movie was the greatest glory moment of the Buchón in the cinema (as well as many other WW2 planes). This classic war movie was the "cause" that today, several Buchones continue flying through the world skies and others have been preserved stored or in museums. Thanks to this film, several Buchones that would have been scrapped shortly were saved at the last moment. For your interest in the history of the legendary Buchón, it is important to remember briefly the story of this film.

The Group Captain (R.) Thomas Gilbert "Hamish" Mahaddie, former RAF pilot, was commissioned by producers Benjamin Fisz and Harry Salzman to look for aircraft for the movie they wanted to film and which was entitled the "Battle of Britain". It was Mahaddie who learned that the Spanish Air Force was in the process of disposing of a number of Hispano HA-1112M1L aircraft.

The Buchones were stored in various states of disrepair in Tablada Airfield Base (Sevilla) in

Spain. After some negotiations by the Air Attaché at the British Embassy in Madrid, the Air Force agreed to sell 18 flyable, 6 taxi-capable and 4 static bolts in order to shoot the film. Besides Spanish Government exonerated to Spitfire Productions (company owned by the Group Captain Hamish Mahaddie that was the man that had to obtaining the aircraft for the film) all expenses incurred during the filming of the aircraft, fuel, maintenance, pilots and groundcrew with the exception of the paint for the aircraft.

The 28 aircraft were purchased for 10821000 pesetas (just over 60000 euros today), having to pay 110000 pesetas more for the repairs that were made in each of them.

According to the Aircraft-Spotter's Film and Television Companion (by Simon D. Beck), the Hispano HA-1112M1L used in the film were (series number in Spanish Air Force):

- Flying aircraft: C.4K- 31, 61, 75, 99, 100, 102, 105, 106, 112, 122, 126, 127, 130, 144, 152, 159, 169 and 170.
- Static aircraft: C.4K- 30, 111, 114 and 154.
- Taxi aircraft: C.4K- 107, 121, 131, 134, 135 and 172.

As a curiosity, we have to comment that the C4K-112 was one of the few two-seater Buchones manufactured, which had been discharged in 1965 while still in flight condition. Another important detail is that 10 aircraft received the C.4J three bladed propellers to achieve a greater resemblance to the German Bf 109.

Not only was the aircraft acquisition negotiated, but it was also agreed that the best pilots for those airplanes in the movie aerial scenes, had to be the most experienced pilots belonging to the Spanish Air Force's Wing 7, which even had combat experience with their beloved Buchones. The same fact happened with the pilots chosen to fly the C.A.S.A. 2111 used in the movie. The selection of pilots began when in May of 1967, the veteran pilot that flew in the Spanish Blue Squadron during WW2, Pedro Santacruz Barceló was hired by the production company to look for pilots able to pilot the Buchón. Pedro Santacruz studied the records of the pilots who had flown the planes, and chose those who had had fewer accidents or incidents.

The superb performance of the Spanish pilots as German pilots and of the HA-1112M1L as the Bf 109E and even as the Hurricane (it was very curious this fact since during the filming it became obvious the lack of airworthy Hurricanes at least three Buchones were painted over to resemble Polish RAF Hurricanes, so they were called "Hurrischmitts") was so spectacular that today, the "Battle of Britain" film is still possibly the best film about Aviation in WW2 ever filmed.

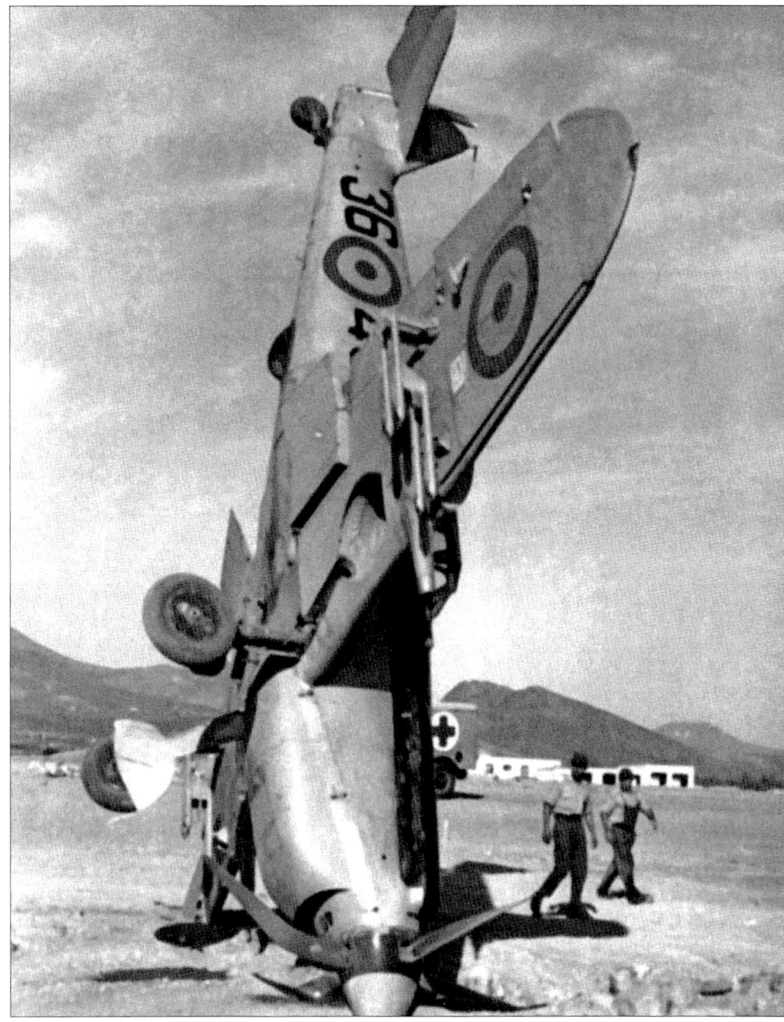

The C.4K-113 with numeral 36-408 belonging to the Mixed Wing 36 suffered an accident on October 22, 1963 in Gando airbase after a training flight, the pilot had problems landing because failed the brake of the left wheel. [By F. Andreu via Juan Arráez]

We must remember that 32 C.A.S.A. 2111 (resembling He 111s in the Transport and VIP flight role) and 2 C.A.S.A. 352L (resembling Ju 52-3ms transports) took part in the film. About these 34 aircraft, Spanish Government informed the British Air Attaché that they agreed to loan 32 C.A.S.A. 2111 and 2 C.A.S.A. 352L to Spitfire Productions for the film sequences; in both types of planes were copies from the German He 111 and Ju 52, although the C.A.S.A. 2111 had Merlin engines in spite of the Jumo. The C.A.S.A. 2111s and C.A.S.A. 352Ls were rented and not sold by the Spanish Government as happened with the HA-1112M1Ls, because they were still being flyed by the Spanish Air Force and therefore could not be purchased for the film company.

The HA-1112M1Ls and the C.A.S.A. 2111s were cared by Spanish Air Force mechanics during the film, both in Spain and United Kingdom.

Important modifications had to be made to the Buchones to make them resemble Messerschmitt Bf 109 Es (this Bf 109 model was used by the Luftwaffe in the 1940's). Evidently the important difference of silhouette between the original engine of the Bf 109 and the one of the HA-1112M1L was outstanding, the other main difference between both airplanes was the wing

The C.4K-104 with numeral 36-407 belonging to the Mixed Wing 36 after suffering an accident while landing in Gando airbase on October 20, 1963. Upon landing the heavy wind led the propeller to hit the ground causing this dive position. The aircraft could be repaired. [By F. Andreu via Juan Arráez]

tips; because the Bf 109 E had squared wing tips and the HA-1112M1L had rounded wing tips. Although the Spanish Air Force at the beginning did not agree with removing the wing tips and fair over the end of the wings, they finally allowed it. Surprisingly, after making the changes in the Spanish aircraft, the performance of the aircraft was good.

Other minor modifications that had to be made in the Buchones were also designed to achieve the maximum similarity between the Spanish and German aircraft. So the Buchones were equipped with fake weapons (fuselage mounted machine guns and wing mounted cannons as the Bf 109 Es had). Besides, the horizontal tail plans were props by struts (since the Bf 109 Fs, the tail plans had no struts). At the moment that all these modifications were made, there was only one last detail left that consisted in the Buchones receiving fictional Luftwaffe units' camouflages and markings.

The filming of the movie took place in Spain (Tablada) and in the United Kingdom. There were many veterans of WW2 who were employed as advisers and specialists, but among them it is necessary to highlight the legendary German ace Adolf Galland, who (according to some source) could even fly in Sevilla a two seater version of the Buchón; also the Luftwaffe pilot Hans Brustellin was a technical adviser for the film. On the part of the Allies, we can highlight aces such as Peter Townsend, Hugh Dowding, "Ginger" Lacey or Robert Stanford Tuck. The relationship between them was of great camaraderie; and it was so important between Adolf Galland and Stanford Tuck that Tuck was the godfather of Andreas (a son of Galland).

After starting the pilots' training in the HA-1112M1L in December 1967, filming began in January 1968, and the first two months were spent in Tablada, with the HA-1112M1L (Bf 109 E) escorting the C.A.S.A. 2111s (He 111). Specifically, filming began at the Tablada airfield in March 1968 (Spanish airbase near Sevilla). Most of the scenes filmed of large bombers formations (He 111) and Bf 109 were filmed there although also Matalascañas beach (Huelva) was used as Dunkirk beach.

Guy Hamilton, the director of the film told the Spanish pilots to forget all the combat tactics they knew because for the film he needed another way to fly differently. So the pilots had to learn to fly for filming in order to achieve the most real airwar film.

During the first two months of the filming in Tablada, the HA-1112M1L piloted by Federico Iglesias, crashed when he lost visibility due to an oil leak. Despite this, the filming went on.

One of the problems raised by the HA-1112M1L was its limited autonomy, causing the filming times to be very short. This was due to the fact that until the moment of filming in the air, it took approximately 40 minutes to take off and train in flight, so they had little time left for real filming time for the movie scenes.

During the simulated combats, it happened that the Spitfires from the first versions could hardly fly and combat against the Buchones with 1800 HP engines reduced to 1610 HP. Because of this, the pilots received orders from the director of the movie to act exactly as he told them and never as they would do in real combat conditions. The tactic that was usually used in simulated combat was to ascend using superpower to "hang" their rivals.

Evidently the airplanes of both sides did not shoot among themselves, but to know who was the winner in the different dogfights it was agreed that when an aircraft was at six o'clock of the foe aircraft for more than 6 seconds, it was considered the winner.

After the filming in Spain, the aircraft moved to the United Kingdom. The 17 flyable HA-1112M1Ls and 2 C.A.S.A. 2111s were flown across the English Channel, then they were certified with British civil registrations. The flight to United Kingdom was done very slowly in order to take care of the venerable aircraft, taking 2 days to finish the journey, during which there were 5 stops (Sevilla, Getafe, Biarritz, Nantes, Jersey, Manston and Duxford). Most of the scenes of the movie were filmed in Duxford (where there were still authentic hangars from the WW2 era) and some in Sothern France because of the bad weather in United Kingdom.

During the filming, each plane flew an average of 125 hours, when the operational life had been calculated in 250 hours.

During the filming of the movie, a new Aerobatic Team flying Buchones was formed thanks to the Spanish pilots that demonstrated the superb performances of the airplane and the mastery of the Spanish pilots. Adolf Galland was amazed and thrilled to see an Aerobatic Team flying the old Messerschmitt. Even the British Fighter Command boss, Sir Hugh Dowding commented that "if the Germans had counted on a couple of squadrons like the Spaniards ... we would have have had more difficulties during the war".

Most of the Buchones that were used during the film were sold to private people. Among these owners we have to remember the well-known pilot Connie Edwards who purchased 9 Buchones that went to USA in 1969.

Another film where probably the Buchón acted again (I never saw this film, but in some sources indicate that the Buchón was used as the Bf 109) was the Anglo-American wartime film "Hanover Street" where the B-25s were the protagonists.

"Piece of cake" was a British TV series (1988) about the life of a Royal Air Force fighter squadron during one of the most dangerous days of the Battle on Britain; and of course the main enemy were the Bf 109s. In this TV series there were three Buchones all with the Rolls-Royce engine that took part trying to resemble the German Bf 109 E. These aircraft flew again in other films like "Memphis Belle".

Another film where the Spanish aircraft returned to bear German insignia was "Memphis Belle" (1990). An American film about the Boeing B-17 bomber of the same name. There were 3 HA-1112M1L, all with the Rolls-Royce engine. The Buchones were painted with knight cross and firing balance at the tail unit. All the HA-1112M1Ls came from Europe.

Another film where the HA-1112M1L flew again with German insignia, was "The Tuskegee Airmen" (1995) or "Escuadrón 332" in Spain, an American film about the famous fighter group with Afro-American pilots in WWII. A lot of the scenes were from wartime footages and the "Memphis Belle" film.

In this interesting film, the Buchón that participated was the C.4K-172 (with civil registration N109GU) and as always resembling the Bf 109 against the Allies.

The Czech film "Tmavomodrý svět" ("Dark Blue World" or " Un mundo azul oscuro " in Spain) from 2001 was another film where the Spanish Bf 109 flew again against the Allies (the C.4K-172 according to the denomination in the Spanish Air Force), specifically this film was about the Czechoslovak pilots in the RAF during WWII. In this film several of the flying scenes were taken from the "Battle of Britain" and retouched digitally.

"Pearl Harbor" is a 2001 film from the USA, where war events are mainly narrated in the Pacific, although a plot in the film takes place during the Battle of Britain; and this is where a Buchon appears. Concretely the airplane made in Spain is the C.4K-77 (with civil register N700E), that appears in combat in front of the British airplanes (4 Spitfires, 1 Hurricane and 1 Sea Hurricane flyable). In this film the HA-1112M1L, again resembled the Bf 109 E.

Another film in which the Buchón returned to be a main actor is "Valkyrie" starring Tom Cruise as Von Stauffenberg. This movie filmed in 2008 tells the events that took place during WW2 in Germany with the attempted murder of Adolf Hitler.

The Buchón (a Hispano HA-1112M1L manufactured in 1959) used in "Valkyrie" is a veteran of the "Battle of Britain" film (the C.4K-102), as it was one of the 27 purchased from the Spanish Air Force by Spitfire Productions Ltd. The plane after the "Battle of Britain" film changed owners several times, finally being sold on to Historic Flying Ltd.

During the film the Buchón can be seen in the scene at the Berlin Tempelhof Airport where a "Bf 109" is inside a hangar. In the film is possible to see the upright V British Merlin V-12

Another picture of the C.4K-113 with numeral 36-408 after suffering the accident when landing. Despite not suffering major damage, the aircraft was finally scrapped. [By F. Andreu via Juan Arráez]

Another photograph with another C.4K crashed in Gando airbase. In this case it is again a C.4K belonging to the Mixed Wing 36. You can appreciate the position of the flaps that are fully extended. [By F. Andreu via Juan Arráez]

The C.4K-113 with coded 36-408 belonging to the 36 Mixed Wing after crashing in the Gando airbase during the landing.[By F. Andreu via Juan Arráez]

engine. Real Messerschmits had an inverted V Daimler-Benz engine. Very few airworthy examples of the Me-109 remain nowadays. This aircraft shown, was flown at the 2008 Duxford Airshow, and is fitted with a British Merlin engine.

One of the last films where the Buchón has returned to fly has been "Dunkirk" (2017) or "Dunkerque" in Spain, resembling of course de Bf 109 with the Luftwaffe camouflage and the badges. As usual, due that there are no real Bf 109 fighter aircraft the HA-1112M1L stood in for those scenes. In the summer of 2016 this Spanish Air Force veteran fighter-bomber was "recruited" to take part in the film. As a curiosity, the Buchón that flew over Dunkirk has its nose painted in yellow to differentiate it from other aircraft, but actually, the German fighters did not use that yellow mark until later in 1940, but the director preferred to paint the nose of the Buchón to make the German aircraft easier to identify. So at last, the UK-based Buchón which represented the German fighter aircraft in the movie air combats again against its old foe the British Spitfire but then, over Dunkirk. Filming was made in several aerodromes such as Lee on Solent on the English coast of the Channel very close to Portsmouth, and the Dutch Hoogeveen.

Recall that the HA-1112M1L is based on the Bf 109 G-2 airframe and that therefore its wings are more similar to those of the F models of the Bf 109 than to the models E. Like during the fighting by Dunkirk the Germans used the Bf 109 E, the differences between the HA-1112M1L and the German plane were evident (the Rolls-Royce Merlin engine was the main guilty) although serving as a great-similar copy of the Bf 109.

The HA-1112M1L along with three Spitfire were the stars of the main air scenes during the film. During the air combats, the Buchón was shot down several times by its British adversaries.

This Buchón which is based at Duxford airfield in England, is a movie star because its credits include beside "Dunkirk", the well-known 1968 "Battle of Britain" movie and the 2008 film "Valkyrie". This Buchón was manufactured in 1959 in the Hispano Aviación factory in the Triana neighborhood (in Sevilla) and while it was flown by the Spanish Air Force, it was based on the El Copero aerodrome(first) then in Tablada aerodrome (in 1968) to be bought by Spitfire Productions in a public auction to use it in the movie "Battle of Britain".

The Buchon today

Fortunately, there are still several Buchones in the world nowadays, including some flyable ones (as we have seen in the chapter about the actor Buchón). Approximately there are about thirty Buchones that have survived until today and much of the blame for this was the " Battle of Britain" movie after which many of the Buchones went to private owners. Today, talking about the existing Buchones, we have to tell that many of them do not have the four blades propellers but three blades propellers instead since in many occasions they have been modified (sometimes changing the cannons in the wings or placing two false cannons on the cowling) in order to look more like the Bf 109. In some of the Buchones (at least 8) the changes have been so important that they have been fitted with the original engine Daimler Benz recovering the characteristic profile of the Messerschmitt aircraft and thus losing its characteristic Spanish profile. These transformed Buchones are particularly difficult to differentiate from their forbears.

MODEL	NUMBER	COUNTRY	STATUS	INFO
HA-1112M1L	c/n 201 C.4K-131 (OO-MAF)	Belgium	Airworthy	
HA-1112M1L	c/n 164 C.4K-114	Canada.	On display	
HA-1112M1L	139 C4K-75 (D-FWME)	Germany	Airworthy	
HA-1112M1L	c/n 156 C.4K-87 (D-FMBB)	Germany	Airworthy	
HA-1112M1L	c/n 234 C.4K-169 (D-FMGZ)	Germany	Airworthy	
HA-1112M1L	c/n 235 C.4K-172 (D-FMVS)	Germany	Airworthy	
Bf 109 E-1	ex-Bf 109 E-3, ex-Spanish AF „C4E-106"	Germany	On display	Ex Condor Legion
HA-1109K1L	C.4J-?	Germany	On display	Rebuilt as Bf 109G-2 with DB605
HA-1109K1L	C.4J-?	Germany	On display	
HA-1112M1L	c/n 194 C.4K-134	Germany	On display	Has been rebuilt with DB 605 engine
HA-1112M1L	c/n 228 C.4K-170 (N170BG)	Germany	On display	Has been rebuilt with DB 605 engine
HA-1112M1L	c/n 213 C.4K-1? (D-FEHD)	Germany	On display	
HA-1109K1L	c/n 56 C.4J-10	Spain	On display	
HA-1112M1L	c/n 211 C.4K-148	Spain	On display	
HA-1112M1L	c/n 67 C.4K-31 (G-AWHE)	United Kingdom	Airworthy	
HA-1112M1L	c/n 172 C.4K-102 (G-AWHK)	United Kingdom	Airworthy	
HA-1112M1L	c/n 133 C.4K-64 (N109FF)	USA	Airworthy	Rebuilt as a Bf 109 G-2 with DB605 engine
HA-1112M1L	c/n 171 C.4K-100 (N76GE)	USA	Airworthy	
HA-1112M1L	c/n 186 C.4K-122 (N109J)	USA	Airworthy	Rebuilt as a Bf 109 E with DB601 engine
HA-1112M1L	c/n 199 C.4K-127 (N109BF)	USA	Airworthy	
HA-1112M1L	c/n unkn C.4K-30	USA	Stored or under restoration	
HA-1112M1L	c/n 120 C.4K-77 (N700E)	USA	Stored or under restoration	Rebuilt with Allison V-1710 and reconfigured 109G-style cowling
HA-1112M1L	c/n 129 C.4K-61 (G-AWHE)	USA	Stored or under restoration	
HA-1112M1L	c/n 137 C.4K-116 (N6109)	USA	Stored or under restoration	
HA-1112M1L	c/n 145 C.4K-105 (N6036)	USA	Stored or under restoration	
HA-1112M1L	c/n unkn C.4K-111	USA	Stored or under restoration	
HA-1112M1L	c/n 166 C.4K-106 (N90607)	USA	Stored or under restoration	
HA-1112M1L	c/n 187 C.4K-99 (N90604)	USA	Stored or under restoration	
HA-1112M1L	c/n 190 C.4K-126 (N90603)	USA	Stored or under restoration	
HA-1112M1L	c/n 195 C.4K-135	USA	Stored or under restoration	
HA-1112M1L	c/n 220 C.4K-152 (N4109G)	USA	Stored or under restoration	
HA-1112M1L	c/n 223 C.4K-154	USA	Stored or under restoration	
HA-1112M1L	c/n 178 C.4K-178	USA	Stored or under restoration	
HA-1112M4L	c/n unkn C.4K-112	USA	Stored or under restoration	Two-seat tandem
HA-1112M1L	c/n 193 C.4K-130 (N90602)	USA	Stored or under restoration	Rebuilt with Allison V-1710 and fitted with Bf 109 G-10 cowling

The HA-1112M1L and HA-1112K1L that exist today, in some cases are on static display in aeronautical museums, belonging to other companies or people who with their effort have managed to keep them in storage (several of them are flyable) and in some cases it is possible that they could take to the air again someday.

It's known that 5 HA-1112M1Ls and 1 HA-1112M4L used in the "Battle of Britain" film sat in storage in Wilson "Connie" Edwards aircraft collection. In 2014, Edwards sold to Boschung Global the six aircraft (one of them was a two seat variant) that is going to restore (although we don't know, airworthy status for these aircraft, as we said, it is possible to see them flying again).

If we want to see the models in their original profile, both the HA-1112K1L and the HA-1112M1L, these are in the Spanish Air Museum (Museo del Aire de España). The HA-1112K1L or C.4J was delivered to the museum in 1971 by the Specialist School in León; while the HA-1112M1L or C.4K was decommissioned in December 1965 with few hours of flight so it is in a great conservation status.

Here we show (table above) a non-definitive list were we can see the ex-Spanish Air Force 109s that exist today based in aviationcorner.net, Aircraft-Spotter's Film and Television Companion and Wikipedia works.

We can see that thanks to the HA-1112M1Ls airframes (we cannot forget that it is a Bf 109 G-2 airframe, it is the suitable airframe to rebuild the aircraft), in several cases it was possible to bring back to life the Bf 109 through a rebuild with an original Daimler Benz engine or other engines that were similar. So thanks to reverse engineering over the Buchónrealistic Bf 109 versions (E or G) have been created. Fortunately today we can enjoy several HA-1112M1Ls and HA-1109K1Ls, as well as a two-seat HA-1112M4L, plus some rebuilt Buchones that have become the legendary Bf 109s. In the United Kingdom Air Show Circuit from time to time, everybody can enjoy some of the last survivors of the Bf 109 mythical saga. In the Imperial War Museum (IWM) Duxford Battle of Britain Airshow celebrated the 23rd and 24th September 2017, took part of the HA-1112 G-AWHK „Black 8" in the role of German Bf 109 (the same actor Buchón that was the star of film „Dunkirk").

The Spanish Bf 109s began their history within the aviation world still in biplane time, coincided with the jets in their first supersonic

Picture taken in 1962 in El Copero airbase where three HA-1112 M1L are ready to take off with Oerlikon rockets and two 20 mm cannons. We can see the colored spinner in the foreground aircraft. [By F. Andreu via Juan Arráez]

flights and even today some of the Buchones fly majestic as worthy descendants of that great aircraft that was and always will be the Messerschmitt Bf 109.

Spanish made bf 109 G-2 derivatives technical info

Based on the superb work of Juan Antonio Guerrero and the technical information of the article written by José Antonio García Pérez, we will commenton the main technical performances of the Bf 109 J (HA-1109 J1L), HA-1112K1L and HA-1112 M1L in this chapter below; although fundamentally and due to its importance, we will devote special attention to the HA-1112M1L. The three aircraft types were based on the Bf 109 G2, so they had similar performances in various aspects.

Finally, we will briefly comment about the performances of the 2 two seat Spanish made Bf 109s: the HA-1110K1L and the HA-1112 M1L. From the HA-1110K1L model only two aircraft were manufactured, which after changing the engine, became the two HA-1112M1L that were manufactured.

Picture of a lonely HA-1112 M1L (C.4K-9) based on El Copero in the Gando airbase during one of his visits to the Canary Islands in 1962. [By F. Andreu via Juan Arráez]

Bf 109 G-2 technical info

We refer very briefly to the performance of the Messerschmitt Bf 109 G-2 because the Spanish aircraft based on the Bf 109, were based in particular on the Bf 109 G-2 model. However, Spain never had Bf 109 G-2 in service, since all Bf 109 derivatives made in Spain had different engines than the German DB 605A.

Length (m)	9,02
Wing span (m)	9,92
Height (m)	2,60
Maximum weight (Kg)	3250
Empty weight (Kg)	2700
Wing surface (m²)	16,20
Engine	DB 605A-1 (1 x 1475 HP)
Maximum speed	640 (at 22,660 ft)
Cruise speed	520 (at 19,685 ft)
Range without external fuel containers (km)	650
Service ceiling (m)	11200
Armament	1 x 20-mm MG151/20 (720 rpm; velocity 1,920 ft.sec) through propeller hub 2 x 7.92-mm MG17 (1,200 rpm; velocity 2,477 ft.sec) above engine
Crew	One

Bf 109 J (HA-1109 J1L) technical info.

Monoplane single-seat fighter-bomber aircraft with a right opening canopy, low trapezoidal wing surface, retractable landing gear and fixed tail wheel.

a) Fuselage: The fuselage was fully metallic semi-monocoque design with an oval cross section. On the underfuselage there was the main rib where the landing gear was attached. The tail wheel was attached to the last rib of the fuselage close to a final fuselage section that was the support for the stabilizers.

b) Wing: two low cantilever half wings attached to the fuselage at three points with steadily decreasing thickness. The wing had a fully metallic single-spar structure with metal flaps and ailerons (both covered with fabric) and automatically opening leading edge slats.

c) Empennage: It was metallic single-spar with static and dynamic compensation and fabric-covered control surfaces.

d) Engine: HS 12Z-89 engine, V12 cylinder in 60° and liquid cooling. 3600 cm3, 1200 HP when taking off (at 2800rpm). The fuel used was 92 octane.

e) Propeller: The first aircraft that flew used a VDM propeller, but the following 24 aircraft mounted since its manufacture an Escher-Wyss propeller. This propeller was metallic and turned to the left. This three bladed propeller had variable pitch and a diameter of 3.1 meters.

f) Landing gear: Two cantilever retractable legs housed in the wing with air/oil shock absorbers and a fixed tail wheel with oil and spring shock absorbers.

g) Flight controls: The aircraft had fixed roll control. The altitude controls were fixed at the front with double steel wires. The steering controls were wires with fixed flaps controls independent of the ailerons.

h) Cockpit: Closed metal structure reinforced with Plexiglas crystals. It had 3 parts, the first fixed with armored front glass (and with two internal handles in the upper angles), the central part has right opening and sliding side windows, the back adapts with its shape to the shape of the fuselage.

Both the central part and the rear part could be ejected while the aircraft was flying.

i) Armament: A HS 404 20 mm cannon with 60 projectiles firing through the axis of the propeller.

j) Technical specifications (HA-1109 J1L):

Length (m)	9,02
Wing span (m)	9,92
Height (m)	2,60
Maximum weight (Kg)	3100
Empty weight (Kg)	2475
Wing surface (m^2)	16,20
Engine	HS 12Z-89 liquid cooling (1 x 1200 HP)
Maximum speed	636 (a 4300 meters)
Cruise speed	520
Range without external fuel containers (km)	600
Service ceiling (m)	11000 (real was 9850 meters)
Armament	1 x HS 404 20 mm cannon through propeller hub
Propeller	Three bladed VDM
Crew	One

HA-1112K1L or C.4J technical info.

Monoplane single-seat fighter-bomber aircraft with a right opening canopy, low trapezoidal wing surface, retractable landing gear.

a) Fuselage: The fuselage was fully metallic semi-monocoque design with an oval cross section. On the underfuselage was the main rib where the landing gear was attached. The tail wheel was attached to the last rib of the fuselage close to a final fuselage section that was the support for the stabilizers.

b) Wing: two low cantilever half wings attached to the fuselage at three points with steadilydecreasing thickness. The wing had a fully metallic single-spar structure with metal flaps and ailerons (covered with fabric) and automatically opening leading edge slats.

The incidence angle was 1° 42 'at the wing root, with 1° average wing sweep and 6° 32' dihedral angle.

c) Empennage: It was metallic single-spar with static and dynamic compensation and fabric-covered control surfaces.

d) Engine:In order to improve the poor performance of the HA-1109 J1L, in this aircraft the in line V-12 liquid cooling Hispano Suiza HS 12Z-17 engine was selected. Its cylinder capacity was 3600 cm3 and it supplied 1300 HP when taking off (at 2650 rpm). The fuel used for this engine was 100/130 octane (we must remember that the fuel used in the HA-1109 J1L was only 92 octane).

e) Propeller: For this aircraft, the propeller chosen was the Three bladed variable pitch De Havilland Hydromatic PD-63-355-1. The diameter of this propeller was 3.12 meters.

f) Landing gear: Two cantilever retractable legs housed in the wing with air/oil shock absorbers and a fixed tail wheel with oil and spring shock absorbers.

g) Flight controls: The aircraft had fixed roll control. The altitude controls were fixed at the front with double steel wires. The steering controls were wires with fixed flaps controls independent of the ailerons.

h) Cockpit: Closed metal structure reinforced with Plexiglas crystals. It had 3 parts, the first fixed with armored front glass (and with two internal handles in the upper angles), the central part has right opening and sliding side windows, the back adapts with its shape to the shape of the fuselage.

Both the central part and the rear part could be ejected while the aircraft was flying.

i) Armament: In this aircraft the armament was improved, so the HA-1112K1L had 2 20 mm Hispano-Suiza HS.404 or 804 cannon with 60 rounds each cannon in a fairing on the wings, then 8 80 mm Oerlikon rockets under the wings. As the armament is the same that the HA-1112M1L, in the Technical info of the aircraft, we will relate the story of the armament of both kind of aircraft.

j) Technical specifications (HA-1112 K1L):

Length (m)	9,13 m
Wing span (m)	9,92 m
Height (m)	2,60 m
Maximum weight (Kg)	3200 kg
Empty weight (Kg)	2475 kg
Wing surface (m^2)	16 m^2
Engine	In line engineV-12 liquid cooling Hispano Suiza HS 12Z-17 (1 x 1400 HP)
Maximum speed	600 km/h
Cruise speed	400 km/h
Range without external fuel containers (km)	690 km
Service ceiling (m)	9800 m (32 200 feet)
Armament	2 x 20 mm Hispano-Suiza HS.404 or 408 cannon (60 rounds per cannon) 8 x 80 mm Oerlikon rockets
Propeller	Three bladed De Havilland Hydromatic PD-63-355-1
Crew	One

HA-1112 M1L or C.4K technical info.

Monoplane single-seat fighter-bomber aircraft with a right opening canopy, low trapezoi-

Shot of the C.4K dubbed "Los Alcores" based on El Copero during one of its visits to Palma de Mallorca in May 1964. Next to the aircraft, the wing tip of another unidentified HA-1112 M1L can be seen. [By F. Andreu via Juan Arráez]

dal wing surface, retractable landing gear and tail wheel.

a) Fuselage: The three types of aircraft were based on the Bf 109 G2, so they had similar performances in various aspects.

The fuselage was fully metallic semi-monocoque design with an oval cross section. On the underfuselage was the main rib where the landing gear was attached. The tail wheel was attached to the last rib of the fuselage close to a final fuselage section that was the support for the stabilizers.

According to one of the pilots of the Buchones, the instruments were the same as those of the Bf 109 G-2, so they were written in German. That is why the Spanish pilots had to get used to them, in some cases converting the German words into other Spanish ones.

b) Wing: two low cantilever half wings attached to the fuselage at three points with steadily decreasing thickness. The wing had a fully metallic single-spar structure with metal flaps and ailerons (covered with fabric) and automatically opening leading edge slats.

The incidence angle was 1° 42 'at the wing root, with 1° average wing sweep and 6° 32' dihedral angle.

The Bf 109, were always characterized by using slats on the wings that increased the lift during the flight, although they had the disadvantage that they increased wing strength. Although it improved the performance of the airplane, this development of the German engineering also increased its cost. In the Hispano Aviación made aircraft, it was necessary to choose if the slats were useful, or if they were unnecessary. In the Spanish-made aircraft, due to its greater complexity, the slats were replaced by small fins that controlled the air flow over the wing and therefore replacing in its function, thanks to this the Buchón in flight was very docile to an optimal cruising speed of 450 km/h and while diving showed good performance (in the anemometer the maximum speed marked was 750 km/h) while when the stalled aircraft was easy to recover fall.

c) Empennage: It was metallic single-spar with static and dynamic compensation and fabric-covered control surfaces.

d) Motor: The various Hispano Aviación aircraft derived from the Bf 109 G-2 evidently had great similarities in many technical aspects, although the presence of the new engine and the obvious change in the aircraft profile (remember that the original engine of Bf 109 had an inverted V while the Spanish airplane had an upright V British Merlin V-12 engine) made piloting a HA-1109 or HA-1112 completely different from piloting a Bf 109.

Thanks to its design, the German engine allowed the placement of weapons through it, but British engine did not allow it. This was the reason why the Spanish aircraft armament had to be very different from the one in the Bf 109s (from which the Spanish aircraft derived).

The 500/45 Rolls-Royce Merlin engine, 27 liter V12 in 60° fitted with single stage one or two speed gearbox (that allowed to recover the power as at sea level about at 3000 meters in the first stage and up to 5500 meters in the second stage) and pressurized liquid cooling, overheat camshaft, 1610 HP (1200kW) maximum boost of 18 psi, of 190 l/h and empty weight of 680 Kg. About the aircraft fuel consumption it must be mentioned that with the Rolls Royce engine matched to the Spanish aircraft, fuel consumption was much higher than expected, so the autonomy was 1 hour and 30 minutes with a flight in economic mode and a consumption about 175 l/h (the Buchón internal fuel tank had 400 liters), despite the fact that the original performance of the British engine was 2 hours and 30 minutes.

Another Buchón characteristic was that at first the propeller turned upside down the opposite that it did in the Bf 109. The German engine turned to the left, while the British engine did it in the opposite direction. Willy Messerschmitt assumed the direction of projects in 1952 (taking the technical direction Ricardo Monet)in his stay in Spain,and worked to solve the modification that the Spaniards had made to "his" airplane (in the German Bf 109 models, this "engine pair" problem had been corrected by making the fuselage withits right side more flattened instead of being a perfect oval). It was necessary to make various corrections to the fuselage and the rudder (the rudder was decaled at an angle that counteracted the Rolls Royce engine torque, although this solution decreased the performance of the aircraft). Anyway, the aircraft were predisposed to do the "caballito" (displacement) to the right in the German models and to the left in the Spanish aircraft, although this problem was controlled by applying the correction. In many occasions the accidents that occurred with the Spanish planes occurred towards the right side, due to the tendency of the pilots to pull the plane to the right to correct the "caballito" to the left.

The aircraft could not be compensated during the flight, it was only possible when it was landed and it was made by folding a small metal sheet on the rudder. When the Buchón began to accelerate, a speed about 110 km/hwas necessary to take off the tail wheel and therefore greatly improve the visibility from inside the cockpit. When the plane was at approximately 200 km/h, the aircraft was ready to take off.

The Rolls Royce engine had 200 HP more than the Bf 109 G-2 Daimler Benz, despite which the Buchon reached only 90% of Bf 109 G-2 performance. That overpowering of the engine had to be handled with great caution, since if all the engine power was used at once, control of the plane was easily lost by the pilot. On the other hand, if the power rise was made very slowly, the take off run lengthened. During the take off of the plane special care was required, since it was done with full power without overpowering normally (only in necessary situations the overpower was used).

One of the problems that had the Bf 109s manufactured in Spain with different engines from the German, was the engine overheating. Although they tried to reduce this problem, it was never completely resolved. In case of high temperatures (remember that most of the operational service of the HA-1109 and the HA-1112 occurred in Sevilla or in Africa), the glycol came out and was spilled by the cowling; being necessary the landing of the airplane as soon as possible.

An engine´s feature was the exhaust gases in the visibility zone of the cockpit, which completely blinded the pilot; so the possibility of being used as a night fighter-bomber disappeared.

e) Propeller: The Bf 109 from the F model had a propeller with shorter blades, which allowed the pilots to lift the tail of the aircraft more, improving the visibility in the take off and landing. But in the C.4K with its four bladed variable pitch Rotol/R 116-4F5/12 propeller, this small advantage for the pilots disappeared completely, due to the more than 3,073 meters in diameter and 192 Kg that this propeller had. Despite this small problem, the propeller fitted perfectly to the engine so, but some light vibrations, it did not had important problems.

The propeller used a simple GRF/7B type gearbox for constant speed and straight gears with right hand traction.

f) Landing gear: Two cantilever retractable legs housed in the wing with air/oil shock absorbers and a fixed tail wheel with oil and spring shock absorbers.

The Buchón was not an easy plane to handle on the ground like the Bf 109 because the visibility from the cockpit was very small (there was a 60° blind zone in the Buchón´s nose due to the engine big size). In addition, it also had

With the signing of the cooperation agreements with the USA signed on September 24, 1953, the USA began to supply modern aircraft to Spain, such as Lockheed_T-33 (in the photograph in Spanish markings) that arrived in Spain in April, 1954. [Public Domain by Darz Mol]

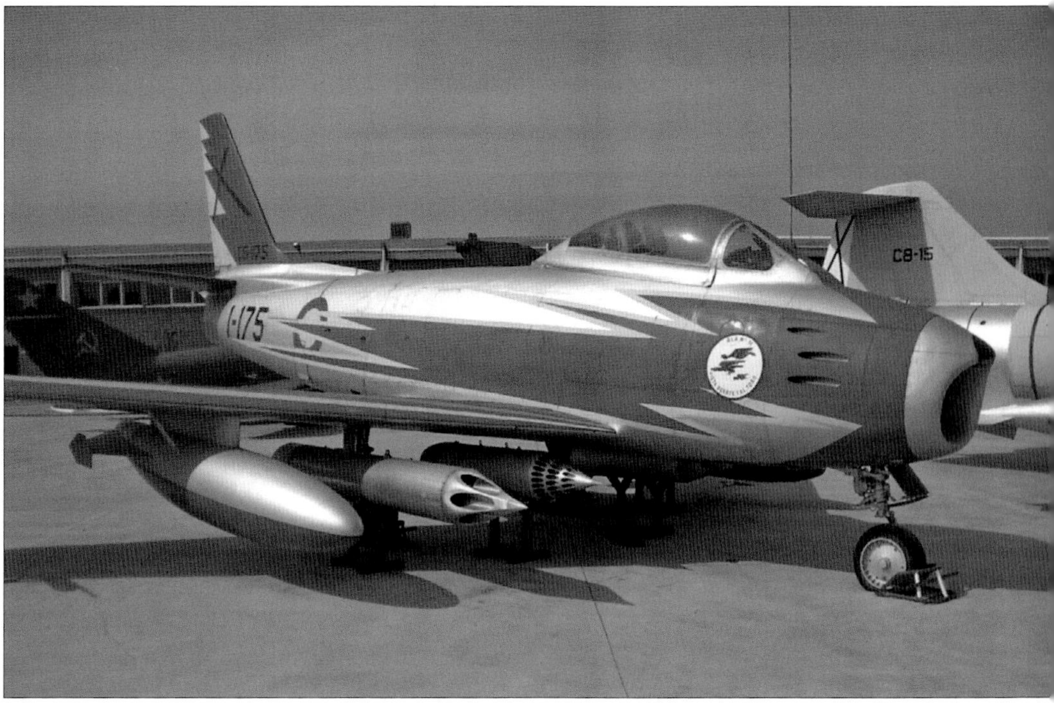
On June 30, 1955, the first F-86F "Sabre" jet arrived at Getafe (Madrid) marking a milestone in the history of Spanish Aviation. This jet was contemporary for a few months (until November 19, 1965) with the HA-1112 M1L in the Spanish Air Force. [Public Domain by Garrapata]

ease to fail the landing gear output, either one leg or both; so on several times caused the plane crash. Also the landing gear was quite weak when it was subjected to lateral stresses, causing numerous accidents. It also did not help that its airbase in El Copero had a ground airstrip that was muddy with the rains, making the aircraft movements on the ground very difficult. Obviously when the Buchón was deployed in the Sidi Ifni and Sahara war, the African airstrips plenty of sand and stones did not help the better handling of the aircraft either.

As the take off had its difficulties, the landing should also be done very carefully, since the airstrip was only visible on both sides of the cockpit, since the engine prevented good forward vision.

g) Flight controls: The aircraft had fixed roll control. The altitude controls were fixed at the front with double steel wires. The steering controls were wires with fixed flaps controls independent of the ailerons.

The instrument panel in the cockpit was manufactured in Spain by a subsidiary company of the Marconi company and was not a high quality panel. As a curiosity, we have to remember that the altimeter had a scale in which the indications were made only every 200 meters. After the Buchones had a more precise altimeter, although globally, the entire instrument panel was very basic, as was the liquid compass that the aircraft carried.

h) Equipment-cockpit: The Bf 109 G2 unlike other Bf 109 Gs, did not have the pressurized cockpit (remember that it was an aircraft designed as reconnaissance aircraft), so the Spanish aircraft had this problem too. Although the Germans solved this deficiency by using oxygen for their pilots, in Spain there were not enough quantities of industrial oxygen, so the one they used was for the modern F-86 jets, leaving the Buchones without that advantage (their role as fighter -bomber allowed this to happen).

Finally, remember that the Buchones were not usually adequately equipped with radiocompass or with oxygen in the cockpit (the latter was not as important due to the use of the aircraft as a fighter-bomber). Only 14 aircraft had the radiocompass installed. As a strengthfor the pilots was the armor cockpit strength which saved many pilots lives in several accidents suffered by these aircraft.

About the VHF communications, the Marconi company had manufactured in Spain 100 devices with 10 stations and maximum range about 100 nautical miles (182 km) for air to ground communication at 10000 feet (3083 meters) and about 200 nautical miles (364 Km) for air to ground communication; those devices were installed in the aircraft. Its official name was the STR 9X VHF radio transmitter-receiver and its simplicity allowed communications between aircraft or between aircraft and bases to be heard by enemy listening services (as happened during the conflict in Sidi Ifni).

i) Other performances: The Buchón, despite his bad reputation when it was on ground, was a superb aircraft when flying. It was very difficult for the aircraft to stall, they could perform diving without problems (although the anemometer only indicated 750 km/h, the speed reached was higher) and allowed aerobatics with extreme ease. Referring to this last fact, the Wing 7 got to create an Aerobatic Team, although finally it was dissolved by the HQ.

j) Armament:

The Spanish Bf 109s armament was different from the Bf 109 G-2 armament, due to the new engine that was installed into the plane. The Rolls Royce engine cylinders were vertical in difference to the Daimler Benz cylinders, this prevented that weapons could be placed on the nose of the plane. At the same time, the larger size of the cowling already worsened the scarce visibility on land that the Bf 109s made in Spain pilots had (both the HA 1109K1L and subsequently the HA 1112M1L).

The first option was to install two 12.7 mm CETME machine guns (at least 10 aircraft had this armament). But this armament was suspended shortly after (in February 1957) and the machine guns were replaced by two 20 mm cannons. The 10 aircraft with machine guns were finally armed with 20 mm cannons.

Faced with this situation, it was decided to place the aircraft armament in a fairing on the wings. The chosen ones were 20 mm Hispano Suiza HS 404 cannons, one of which was placed in each wing. Originally, these guns had a curious history, as they arrived in Spain in the summer of 1941 in the merchant ship "San Diego". This ship had an armament shipment (that included 165 HS 404 cannons and 123,176 rounds) with destination to the French forces deployed in North Africa and due to a failure it had to go to the Bilbao harbor and was immediately seized. The cannons were split between the Spanish Ground Forces and the Spanish Air Force, which received 55 20 mm Hispano Suiza HS 404 cannons. Subsequently, new similar cannons were bought, although this time they were 20 mm Hispano Suiza HS 804. The main difference between both cannons was that the HS 804 had higher firing rate (840/minute compared to 780/minute in the HS 404), although the upload system was also electromagnetic in the HS 804 and pneumatic in the HS 404. They were also different in the magazine, since the HS 804 had it in cassette and the HS 404 in drum.

The 20 mm Hispano Suiza HS 404 cannons were mounted on HA 1112M1L with fuselages numbered up to C.4K-50; and even some aircraft left the Hispano Aviation facilities without cannons.

The cannons installation on the wings lead to a new problem for the Hispano Aviación engineers (in Sevilla), because in order to install the cannons it was necessary to cut the wing spar (remember that the original Bf 109G did not have guns on the wings). Thanks to the change of the slats by the fins, it was gained a little more space for the installation of the guns on the wings. It was necessary to add a guide vanes on the upper wing surface to channel the airflow that was altered by the cannons despite the fairness which they had been installed.

The cannons were very neatly packaged within the wing and did not require blisters to accommodate the breeches and ammunitions feed like the MG FF installation in the Bf 109 E for example.

The two 20 mm Hispano Suiza cannons has a total length of 2115 cm, 12 flutes at 7°, rate of fire 710-840 rpm with 120 round disintegration link belt; initial projectile speed 840 m/sg and a total weapon weight about 52 Kg.

According to sources, the verification for the combat procedure required several steps: flaps up, compensator in the right mode, confirm landing gear up, fuel pumps on, tail wheeled blocked and propeller pitch forward.

In addition to the 2 powerful 20 mm cannons, the Buchón also had 8 Oerlikon HSS R-80 rockets attached to four Pilatus type MMM double launchers under the wings, with conver-

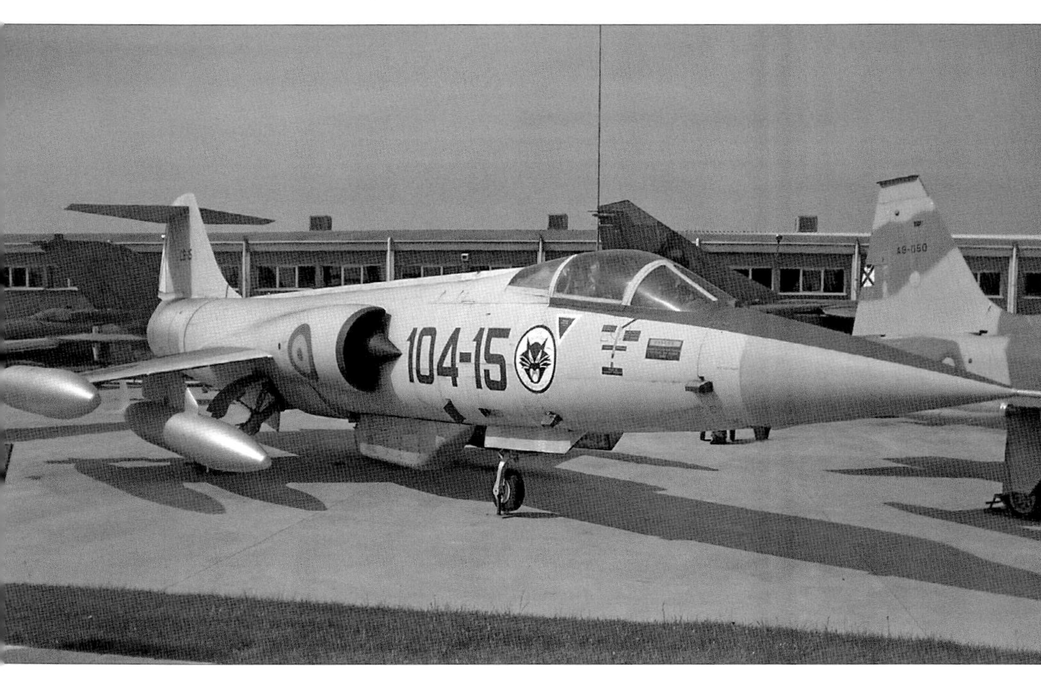

Another jet that was contemporary with the HA-1112 M1L in the Spanish Air Force was the F-104G "Starfighter" that arrived in January 1965. The F-104G of the photo is in the Air Museum. [Public Domain by Garrapata]

HA-1109 K in Luftwaffe camouflage for the "Battle of Britain" movie ground scenes. This aircraft was modified deleting the air intakes in both sides of the under nose and bearing the swastica in the tail. [Courtesy of Juan Arráez]

gence between 400 and 500 m. Rockets were manufactured under license by MMM (Manufacturas Metálicas Madrileñas Sociedad Anónima) and weighed 10 Kg, with a warhwead of 6 Kg and a range about 10 Km.

While the rockets were very precise weapons thanks to their speed and straight trajectory, the cannons were not so reliable, since they jammed so often.

There were also tests to know the performance of the Spanish manufactured S-2 and later with the improved S-6 rockets, which were placed on the rails used for Oerlikon rockets making only a few small changes in the rocket hooking system.

The first test with the S-6 rocket was made on December 28, 1960 from 300 meters height and a 30 degrees diving. Until June 1961, only 77 S-6 rockets were fired from the HA-1112M1L.

The aircraft had a QBI reflex gun sight and a rocket selector to shoot them. Obviously, the Slugs were not first-class fighter jets, but within their role as fighter-bombers, they can be considered as very valid aircraft despite their obsolescence since birth.

After the first combat experience in Sidi Ifni, Hispano Aviación engineers began to develop a new weapon for the HA-1112M1L taking advantage of the hook system developed to install the drop tank. In this case they thought about a grenade launcher that launches small anti-person bombs from a small container placed under the Buchón´s belly. Finally this grenade launcher, as it happened to other ideas destined to increase the Buchón´s performance, were definitively abandoned.

k) Drop tanks

The history of the design and manufacture of drop tanks to allow the direct flight of the Buchones to the Spanish West Africa, deserves a small chapter of its own.

As we have said, the Spanish Air Force HQ, after deciding shortly before Christmas 1957 that the Buchones had to be sent to the Gando airbase after stopping at Sidi Ifni and El Aaiún, they started three frantic work days in the Hispano Aviación facilities in Triana neighborhood (Sevilla).

The orders clearly indicated that a drop tank with a mínimum capacity about 400 liters should be ready in 24 hours. Initially, Hispano Aviación engineers, led by Jesús Salas Larrazabal, thought that a F-86 jet drop tank of the from the nearby Morón de la Frontera airbase (Sevilla) could be used. The drop tank should be housed in the Buchón´s belly, after several settings.

Salas Larrazabal, due to the short time Jesús Salas Larrazabal had to get the Buchón to fly by itself to Africa, did not wait for the F-86 drop tank to be sent to them but started with his work group to manufacture a drop tank for the Buchón. At 8:00 pm on the first work day, they worked with the pieces that were going to be used to join the drop tank to the Buchón. After the first night, Salas Larrazabal was already working with three possible ways for the right matching between the drop tank and the Buchón. At 2.00 the next day (they still had less than 24 hours of work) a first attempt (unsuccessful) of matching the newly manufactured drop tank in a Buchón was made. Three hours later, (after 20 work hours) the Buchón was ready to receive the Sabre drop tank; although this never arrived (from the Morón de la Frontera airbase it was reported that it was impossible to send it).

Faced with the impossibility of receiving the F-86 drop tank, Salas Larrazabal and his team were allowed to have another 24 work hours, but now this extra time was to manufacture a new improvised auxiliary fuel drop tank (from the beginning of the manufacturing). So he began a second work day without stopping for the design and manufacture of a non-drop tank (initially the HQ desire was a non-drop tank so it can be used for a ferry flight between Sevilla and Sidi Ifni and not to be used in combat missions). The effort in Salas Larrazabal working group in the Hispano Aviación facilities was high. After 24 work hours, they achieved their goal: a non-drop tank for the Buchón. The idea

A Spanish "Luftwaffe Schwarm" waiting for the next take off. Four HA-1112 M1Ls lined up during the filming of the "Battle of Britain" movie. [By JM Ochoa via JM González]

was to transfer the fuel from an external tank to the main tank in the fuselage; the external tank was placed under the fuselage and was pressurized with the excess air from the other aircraft instruments. For the second day without stop, the engineers and workers managed to fulfill their duty and managed to install the non-drop tank in the Buchón.

But before 48 hours had passed since the order received by Salas Larrazabal, and when they thought they had finished the work, they received a messenger from the Air Ministry who told them. "The drop tank has to be jettisoned in flight: you have 24 more hours". Again the work began, the tank clamps were cut and a system was created so that it would allow the pilot to release the tank (by means of a mechanical control with hinges). Among the different tank types that had been evaluated during the previous day (three pressurized tanks were built with 2 mm aluminum sheets with two support braces, each one had a different capacity), it was finally chosen the elongated drop tank with a final truncated cone section instead of a cylindrical one with a capacity of 400 liters and which was a few centimeters from the ground. After those last 24 hours, the drop tank was ready to be tested in flight.

To ensure that the fuel was sucked up to the engine, a fuel pump was not used, but air was diverted under pressure from the instrument system to increase the drop tank pressure so that the fuel passed only from the drop tank to the main tank.

The drop tank did not have any indicator showing the fuel left. The fuel transfer from the drop tank to the aircraft tank had to be done only thanks to the knowledge and experience of the pilot but with the risk that the tank could be leaking and spilling. The pilots were ordered not to wait for the main tank to be emptied to begin using the drop tank, since if the transfer failed, the aircraft was in danger of running out of fuel. The fuel movement inside the drop tank was evident every time the pilot turned the HA-1112M1L.

These 72 work hours without stop in the Hispano Aviación facilities were a real achievement and a magnificent example of the tenacity and discipline with which Salas Larrazabal's work group faced such an important challenge despite the continuous counter-orders received. With good humor, workers had participated in the manufacture of the improvised auxiliary fuel drop tank, called those three days as "Operation Cucumber".

Immediately a Buchón was prepared with the drop tank to verify that the work had been carried out correctly. The Hispano Aviación pilot Fernando de Juan Valiente was the one who tested the drop tank in flight on El Copero with good results. Subsequently, several more tank drop tests were carried out, and even a flight made over Andalusia, covering the same distance as Sevilla-Sidi Ifni.

Once the drop tank was qualified as suitable for use in service after being baptized as "big cucumber" it was installed in the Buchones that would be sent to Africa.

A "little cucumber" with less fuel capacity was also manufactured that was used for reconnaissance missions.

l) Technical specifications (HA-1112 M1L):

Length (m)	9,13 m
Wing span (m)	9,92 m
Height (m)	2,60 m
Maximum weight (Kg)	3.330 kg
Empty weight (Kg)	2656 kg
Wing surface (m²)	16 m²
Engine	1× V-12 liquid cooling Rolls-Royce Merlin 500-45 (1 x 1400 HP)
Maximum speed	665-675 km/h
Cruise speed	400 km/h
Landing speed	179,5 km/h
Stall speed	160 km/h
Range without external fuel containers (km)	765 km
Maximum fuel capacity	420 liters
Maximum endurance	1h 30 minutes
Service ceiling (m)	9800 m -10200 m
Climb speed	16,3 m/s
Flaps down speed	300 km/h
Take off distance	600 m
Landing distance	700 m
Armament	2 x 20 mm Hispano-Suiza HS.404 or 408 cannon (60 rounds per cannon) 8 x 80 mm Oerlikon rockets
Propeller	four bladed Rotol
Crew	One

HA-1110 K1L or C.4J technical info.

Monoplane, two-seat trainer aircraft based on the HA-1112K1L.

The studies for a HA-1112K1L two-seat version began in 1950, with the problem that the Hispano Aviación engineers did not have German documentation about the Bf 109 two-

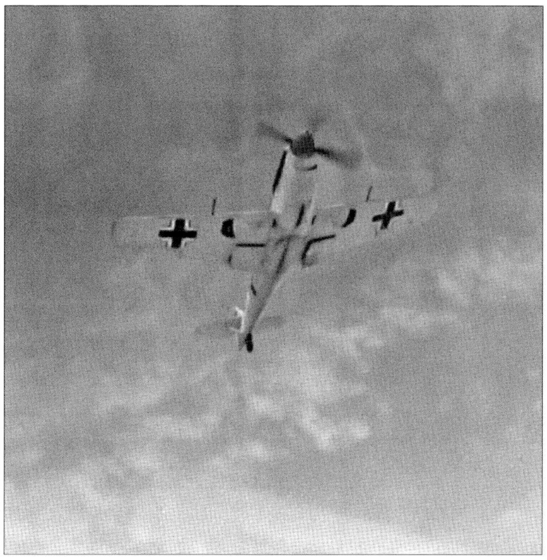

A "Luftwaffe Rotte" flying high in May 1968 during the training for the filming of the "Battle of Britain" movie. [By JM Ochoa via JM González]

seater versions. On March 7, 1952, the contract between the Air Ministry and Hispano Aviación for the delivery to the Spanish Air Force of two two-seat C.4J with engine and propeller. The Ministry paid 1984106 pesetas to Hispano Aviación for the two aircraft.

In 1952 work began on a two-seat trainer version, the HA-1110-K1L with the Hispano Suiza 12Z-17 engine. The two two-seat C.4J aircraft were obtained from the transformation of the last two one-seat aircraft of the 1943 contract.

The HA-1110-K1L was really good, with a canopy that had 360° of field of view, improving the performance of the aircraft in training duties. Only two were ever manufactured, which was a low amount to get an adequate pilots training guided by a trainer, forcing in many cases that the pilots had to do their first flight in the HA-1112K1L alone.

In order to improve the training performance, these two aircraft lacked of armor plating, radio or armament.

Although it was dubbed "two seat Tripala", in the Spanish Air Force, the two seat trainer was called C.4J, the same as the one seat fighter-bomber HA-1112 K1L.

Length (m)	9.1 m
Wing span (m)	9,92 m
Height (m)	2,60 m
Maximum weight (Kg)	2891 kg
Empty weight (Kg)	2375 kg
Wing surface (m^2)	16 m^2
Engine	In line engineV-12 liquid cooling Hispano Suiza HS 12Z-17 (1 x 1400 HP)
Maximum speed	650 km/h (7000 meters)
Cruise speed	480 km/h (6000 meters)
Landing speed	180 km/h
Take off speed	190 km/h
Take off distance	390 meters (with flaps)
Range without external fuel containers (km)	650 km
Maximum fuel capacity	423 liters
Maximum endurance	1h 45 minutes
Service ceiling (m)	10000 m
Armament	None
Propeller	Three bladed De Havilland Hydromatic PD-63-355-1
Crew	Two

HA-1112 M4L or C.4K technical info.

Monoplane two-seat trainer aircraft based on the HA-1112 M1L.

There were only two manufactured aircraft of this model, in both cases they were conversions of the two seat tandem trainer HA-1110 K1L. These aircraft were re-engined with the Merlin engine. On December 31, 1957 both aircraft were already being used in flight and on January 28, 1958 the first two seat tandem trainer HA-1112 M4L was officially accepted by the Spanish Air Force. The second HA-1112 M4L was accepted on June 24, 1959 by the Spanish Air Force.

These training aircraft were sent to Wing 7 in "El Copero" and then to the Wing 47 in Tablada. In any case, two aircraft were too few to satisfy the imperative need to give adequate training to the new pilots. This aircraft was manufactured with the hope that the trainer would help avoid the frequent accidents in the single-seaters due to poor visibility while taxiing. The denomination of both airplanes was C.4K-35 and C.4K-112 (during the time that these airplanes were HA-1110-K1L, they did not get to have official numeration in the Spanish Air Force).

Both HA-1112 M4Ls lacked armament, armor plating or radio. The canopy had 360° field of view, improving the aircraft training performance. This two-seat tandem trainer had indeed better performance than the Bf 109 G12 (the Bf 109 G trainer version).

The two seat Buchón was more aerodynamically clean and lack of armament, so piloting it was not as difficult as in single-seater. In addition it was also faster than the HA-1112M1L about 70 km/h.

In the Spanish Air Force, the two seat trainer was called C.4K, the same as the one seat fighter-bomber HA-1112 M1L.

Length (m)	9,13 m
Wing span (m)	9,92 m
Height (m)	2,60 m
Maximum weight (Kg)	2760 kg
Empty weight (Kg)	2400 kg
Wing surface (m^2)	16 m^2
Engine	1× V-12 liquid cooling Rolls-Royce Merlin 500-45 (1 x 1400 HP)
Maximum speed	745 km/h
Cruise speed	400 km/h
Landing speed	179,5 km/h
Stall speed	160 km/h
Range without external fuel containers (km)	765 km
Maximum fuel capacity	400 liters
Maximum endurance	1h 30 minutes
Service ceiling (m)	9800 m -10200 m
Take off distance	600 m
Landing distance	700 m
Armament	None
Propeller	four bladed Rotol
Crew	Two

Buchón's camouflage and markings

When leaving the Hispano Aviación facility in Sevilla, the HA-1112M1had a bluish priming paint, which was quickly replaced by the final paint.

The color in which the Buchones were painted since they began their story in the Spanish Air Force at its base in El Copero, was the cobalt blue (blue nº 9). It is curious the story why this was the color chosen for these fighter-bombers despite not being unusual in the camouflage of combat aircraft.

The aircraft that left the factory on San Jacinto Street were painted blue. According to some source, the reason for choosing this color was because Major Comas had great friendship with the Peugeot car dealership owner in Sevilla; his friend was the one who provided him with enough paint to paint the Buchones in his Unit. So the paint used was created to be used on cars, not on aircraft that would fly more than 500 km/h.

According to another version, the name of the color as blue Peugeot was due to the fact that one of the Hispano Aviación executives had a Peugeot car with the same color.

On the cobalt blue paint (or Peugeot blue as it was also known) the Spanish badges were painted in six positions (on each side of the fuselage and above and below each wing) and the Saint Andrew's Cross on the tail of the plane. The Spanish badge consisted of a circle with the three colors of the Spanish national flag: red in the outside ring-yellow in the middle ring-red in the inner disc). The St. Andrew's Cross, represents the martyrdom to which the apostle was subjected and is used in Spain dates back to the time of the marriage of Joan of Castile with Philip "the Beauty", being attached to the shield of the Burgundy's Cross, region where Saint Andrew is the patron, as a tribute to her husband. The St. Andrew's Cross continued to be used in the Spanish Air Force aircraft tail until today.

In addition, as commented during the text, the pilots of the Buchones enjoyed the privilege of being able to customize their airplanes, baptizing their airplanes with different names like "Mapi", "Chiqui", "Checa", "El Teobal", "Pepi" , "Loreto", "El Copero", "El Sequeira", "La Cascajera", "El Mojama", "Inés", "El Trobal", "El Toruño", "Julía", "Los Alcores" or "Con dos...".

Possibly due to the origin of the aircraft painting, when the Buchones flew (and especially after their stay in the Sahara desert), the painting was being torn off in some areas of the aircraft, forcing them to paint more damaged areas with small painting patches. All this motivated the appearance of the Buchones´ color became a blue worn with various shades, which in some cases has been confused with a gray or even various greenish tones.

The numbers in the fuselage and the Spanish badges did not show the wear suffered by the Buchón painting, possibly for two reasons: they were painted with a better quality paint (suitable for use in airplanes) and they were repainted more frequently.

With reference to the numbers painted on aircraft fuselages (numerals), 71 was painted on the aircraft fuselage when the 71 Fighter-bomber Tactical Squadron was not subordinated to any other unit. At the beginning, the numbers were painted black, but a short time later they were painted with a white edge to improve their visibility.

HA-1112 M1L "yellow 15" in Luftwaffe markings was one of the 28 Buchones that Spanish Air Force agreed to sell in order to film the "Battle of Britain" movie. [Courtesy of Warbirds]

When the Wing 7 was created, the 71 was changed to the 7. After the formation of the 72 Fighter-bomber Tactical Squad, the numerals used by both this Squadron and the 71 Squadron were indistinctly even and odd mixed numbers (not were reserved the pairs for the 72 Squadron and the odd for the 71 Squadron).

A curiosity with regard to the numerals used by the Buchones, was the use of the number 0 by the commander Comas (71-0), since that number has never been used in Spanish Air Force t.

The HA-1112M1L that were deployed in the 364 Squadron (based in Gando) initially used two identification numbers: the aircraft number in the Spanish Air Force (C.4K-104 as an example) and another concerned to the Wing to which they belonged with 2 numbers on one side and two numbers on the other side of the Spanish badge (36-47 as an example). But later, there were two numbers on one side of the Spanish badge and three on the other side (36-407 as an example). The Spanish Air Force number was painted in the tail (C.4K-104 as an example) and the numeral in the fuselage (36-47 as an example).

Since 1959, they began to assess the possibility of changing the paint color to the Wing 7 Buchones, and between 1962-1963 they went from having a cobalt blue color to having aluminum color in the aircraft upper areas and light blue in the lower areas.

Initially the spinners in the Buchones were painted black when leaving the Hispano Aviación factory, although different colors were used later. Since the creation of the Fighter-bomber Wing 7 on March 2, 1959, in order to differentiate the HA-1112M1Ls belonging to the 71 Fighter-bomber Tactical Squadron from the aircraft belonging to the 72 Fighter-bomber Tactical Squadron, the spinners in the 71 Squadron were painted split black and red (the tip) the spinners in the 72 Squadron were painted split black and yellow (the tip). However it isalso known that the HA-1112M1Ls had the spinners painted split black and red or yellow or white during their service time in the Spanish Air Force, but the white color did not belong to any Squadron, but corresponded with the HQ Squad. Even more, a single aircraft (the Fighter-bomber Wing 7 chief Buchón had its spinner painted in three three colors, the outside being white, the yellow in the middle and the red inside).

Later and thanks to its role like actor, the Buchones were seen with diverse German camouflages from diverse WW2 periods (depending on the movie) and even with British camouflage (Hurrischmitt in "Battle of Britain" movie). Currently, the Buchones that still take part in aerial festivals show Luftwaffe camouflage (with or without swastika depending on the aircraft).

Although in this chapter we deal with the Buchon's camouflage, we must remember its predecessor, the HA-1112K1L (C.4J) that was painted in medium bluish gray color and its numbering was in black.

Annexes

Annex 1: Hispano Aviación

The Hispano Aviación Sociedad Anónima (H.A.S.A.) and Construcciones Aeronáuticas Sociedad Anónima (C.A.S.A.) werethetwomainaeronautical industries in Spain after WW2. In both companies, the aircraft were built with German patent in the postwar period.

The Hispano Aviación origins date back to a company called "J. Castro, Sociedad en Comandita, Hispano-Suiza de Automoviles", which was founded in 1902. That company manufactured engines and cars, although it was finally renamed "La Hispano-Suiza, Fábrica de Automóviles, S.A." when changing ownership. From 1915 the new company began to manufacture aviation engines. The company had a great success, managing to sell a large number of engines all over the world. Due to that great success, the company was divided into a factory dedicated to the production of military equipment (the Hispano Guadalajara) and another called the Hispano Aircraft.

During the Spanish Civil War, the Republican side decided to dismantle the factory in Guadalajara and moved it to La Rabassa (Alicante) to prevent it from being captured by the National side. It was in this facility where the Polikarpov R-Z, R-5 and I-16 were mounted. Meanwhile, the Hispano facilities in Sevilla (in territory controlled by the National side) was installed in the neighborhood of Triana (Sevilla) where the Fiat Cr.32 aircraft began to be repaired. At the end of the Spanish Civil War in 1939, the facilities machines in La Rabassa were moved to Sevilla where the manufacturing under license of the Fiar CR.32 Quater (known in Spain as HA-132L (4)) began.

The Air Minister General Juan Yagüe proposed a great modernization plan in the Spanish Air Force. This plan highlighted the importance of aircraft manufacturing in Spain, whose aeronautical industry was outdated compared to other European countries. Between April and May 1941, two laws in which the terms that the contestants companies should offer to become the most important Aircraft company in the Spanish aeronautical industry in the next year were created. They should be anonymous companies with 2/3 of private capital (of which at least 75% should be Spanish) and 1/3 of state capital. Thus, on June 23, the Hispano Aviación Sociedad Anónima was created (since Hispano Suiza was semi-nationalized in 1943), and had its headquarters in Triana (Sevilla). The share capital was 30 million pesetas (180000 euros today), of which 20 million were contributed by Hispano Suiza and 10 million by the Spanish State (specifically the Industry National Institute). After acquiring the licenses to build several German aircraft (Bf 109 G-2, He 111 H) the Hispano Aviación S.A. (HASA) had to manufacture the Bf 109 G-2 (after winning the contest in order to manufacturing of fighters) and Construcciones Aeronáuticas Sociedad Anónima (CASA) had to manufacture the He 111 (after winning the contest for the manufacture of bombers). On November 8, 1943, the order to manufacture 200 Bf 109 G-2 aircraft (its exact name was Bf 109 Ga-2) with 12Z-89 Spanish-made engines was given.

As we related in the text, finally in the Hispano Aviación, the HA-1109 and HA-1112 models were mainly manufactured, as well as some two-seater models in small numbers.

The history of the Hispano Aviación continued with the manufacture of various aircraft among which the superb Ha-200 "Saeta" designed in 1955 by Willy Messerschmitt (it was the first jet manufactured in Spain), until 1971 when the Hispano Aviación was absorbed by its "sister company" Construcciones Aeronáuticas Sociedad Anónima (CASA).

Annex 2: Spanish made Bf 109 G-2 derivatives production

In this list we try to show to the readers all the Spanish made Bf 109 G-2 derivatives. We have to remember that the total number of aircraft manufactured is not the same as the total sum in the following table. The reason is that some aircraft were reengined and appear as different models of aircraft, such as the 25 HA-1109 J1L that were finally transformed into HA-1112 K1L.

Model	Year	Engine	H.P.	Number
Bf 109 E-1	1941	HS 12-Z-89	1300	1
HA-1109 J1L or C-12	1947	HS 12-Z-89	1300	25
HA-1112 K1L or C.4J	1951	HS 12-Z-17	1400	38. The 25 HA-1109 J1L later were rebuilt as HA-1112 K1L
Two seat HA-1110 K1L or C.4J	1953	HS 12-Z-17	1400	2
HA-1109-M1L	1956	Merlin 500-45	1650	1 It was a HA-1109 K1L rebuilt with Merlin engine
Two-seat HA-1110-M1L	Never manufactured	Merlin 500-45	1650	
Two-seat HA-1111-K1L	Never manufactured	HS 12-Z-17	1400	With fuel tanks in the wing-tips
HA-1112 M1L or C.4K	1956	Merlin 500-45	1650	171
Two-seat HA-1112 M4L	1958	Merlin 500-45	1650	2 1 brand new, the other one was a HA-1110 K1L with new Merlin engine
Total serviceable aircraft				235

The following data refer to the years after the Buchones debut (all aircraft are HA-1112 M1L, except 2 that were two seat trainers HA-1112 M4L) and the Buchón discharged years, are based on the superb work by Carlos Pérez San Emeterio.

YEAR	NEW IN SERVICE	RETIRED	TOTAL IN SERVICE	SERVICE NUMBER
1956	2		2	C.4K- 7,8
1957	19		21	C.4K-2-6, 9-22
1958	56	9	68	C.4K- 23-77, 79
1959	50	10	108	C.4K- 80-127, 78, 129
1960	41	2	147	C.4K-128, 130-169
1961	3	18	132	C.4K-170-172
1962		6	126	
1963		12	114	
1964		44	70	
1965		48	22	
1966		22	0	
TOTAL	171	171		

All the Buchones discharged from active service were due to accidents except those that occurred in 1964 (due to the 72 Squadron disbandeing), 1965 (when the Buchones were discharged because their obsolescence) and in 1966 (when the last Buchones that still flew were sent to storage).

As we can see, the total number of Buchones built was 171, although the accepted number is 172. Possibly (although it is not possible to confirm it) the plane 172 could be the C.4K1. The C.4K1 does not exist, so it is very possible that the C.4K1 was a HA-1109 M1L without armament that was subsequently modified.

Annex 3: Spanish Air Force ranks and equivalences

We recall in this annex the equivalences between the ranks of the Spanish Air Force, USAAF and RAF.

EJÉRCITO DEL AIRE	USAAF	RAF
Capitán General	General (5 stars)	Marshal of the RAF
General del Aire	General (4 stars)	Air Chief Marshal
Teniente General	Liutenant-General	Air Marshal
General de División	Major-General	Air Vice-Marshal
General de Brigada	Brigadier-General	Air Commodore
Coronel	Colonel	Group Captain
Teniente Coronel	Lieutenant-Colonel	Wing Commander
Comandante	Major	Squadron Leader
Capitán	Captain	Flight Lieutenant
Teniente	First Lieutenant	Flying Officer
Alférez	Second Lieutenant	Pilot Officer
	Flight Officer	Warrant Officer
Suboficial Mayor	Master Sergeant	Flight Sergeant
Subteniente	Technical Sergeant	Sergeant
Brigada	Staff Sergeant	
Sargento	Corporal	Corporal
Cabo 1°		Leading Aircraftman
Cabo	Private 1st Class	Aircraftman 1st Class
Soldado	Private 2nd Class	Aircraftman 2nd Class

Bibliography

Abellán García-Muñoz, Juan. Galería de aviones de la Guerra Civil española (1936-1939). Ministerio de Defensa. 2003.

Ala 46. 50 años de historia 1965-2015. Ministerio de Defensa. 2015.

Almena Editorial.

Arráez Cerdá, Juan.

Arráez Cerdá, Juan. Les Espagnols de la Luftwaffe. Les Escadrilles Bleues. Ciel de Guerre 18. 2010.

Arráez Cerdá, Juan. Les Espagnols de la Luftwaffe. Les Escadrilles Bleues. Ciel de Guerre 19. 2011.

Aviationcorner.net. Ricardo Sanabria.

Aviationcorner.net. Fernando Llorente.

Aviationcorner.net. Juan M. González.

Aviationcorner.net. J.M. Ochoa Cao

Aviationcorner.net. Francisco Andreu

Aviationcorner.net. José A. Rubio

Aviones para España. info@aeropinakes.com

Beaman, John R, ; Campbell, Jerry. Messerschmitt Bf 109 in action Part 1. Squadron Signal Publications. 1980

Beaman, John R. Messerschmitt Bf 109 in action Part 2. Squadron Signal Publications. 1983,

Breffort, Dominique; Jouineau, André. Messerschmitt Me 109 from 1943 to 1945. Histoire & Collections. 2002.

Caballero, Carlos; Guillén, Santiago. Escuadrillas azules en Rusia. Historia y uniformes. Almena. 1999.

Canales Torres, Carlos. Las campañas del Sáhara (1957-1958). Ristre. 2008.

Canales, Carlos; del Rey, Miguel. Breve historia de la guerra de Ifni-Sáhara. Nowtilus. 2010.

De Madariaga Fernández, Rafael. Las escuelas de caza Reus y Morón.Revista Aeroplano 1997 nº 15.

De Ugarte y Riu, Manuel. Entre Junkers y Buchones. Galland books. 2008.

De Witt, Norm; Humphries, Julian. Czechs mules and Spanish pigeons (article).

Fernández-Coppel Larrinaga, Jorge. La Escuadrilla Azul. La Esfera de los Libros. 2006.

García Bermúdez, Carlos. Extracto de conferencia del Piloto de Buchón realizada en enero de 2011 en L´Aeroteca. Barcelona.

Garcia Perez, Jose Antonio. El "Messer" español. El C-4K. Revista Aeroplano 1997 nº 15.Gil Martínez, Eduardo Manuel. Spanish Air Force durin World War II. Germany´s hidden Ally?. Kagero. 2019.

González Serrano, José Luis. Los derivados hispanos del Bf 109. Autoedited 2016.

Guerrero, Juan Antonio. Alas de Andalucía 1915-2015. Un siglo de aviones andaluces. Universidad Internacional de Andalucía. 2015.

Guerrero, Juan Antonio. Años 50. Vástago final.Revista Aeronáutica Andaluza nº 26. Enero 2013.

Guerrero, Juan Antonio; Clemente Esquerdo, José. Innovación y desarrollo de la aeronáutica en Andalucía. Fundación Corporación Tecnologíca de Andalucía. Octubre 2014.

https://flaps-aviacion-aviation-luftfahrt.blogspot com/2010/08/hispano-aviacion-haa-1112-buchon.html

http://elhangardewingsofwar.blogspot.com/2012/07/el-ultimo-combate-del-messer.html

http://www.elgrancapitan.org/foro/viewtopic php?f=60&t=19285&start=30

http://www.hispaviacion.es/los-reactores-del-ejercito-del-aire-espanol-la-evolucion-del-poder-aereo/ por Martín Crespo, Luis.

http://www.aviadoresvirtuales.org/index ... ils&did=66

http://www.diariodeavisos.com/2013/08/aterrizaje-buchon-en-playa/

http://elsitiodejactres.blogspot.com/2013/07/hispano-aviacion-sa-ha-1112-buchon-y.html

La aviación en el cine. La Batalla de Inglaterra.Revista Avión nº 285. Noviembre 1969.

Clemente Ezquerdo, José. Base aérea de Tablada. Revista Aeroplano 1994, nº 12.

Medina, Manuel. "Buchones en el Sahara"(Los C.4K Españoles en combate). Revista "FAM, Historia Militar" número 1.

Mermet, Jean Claude; Ehrengardt, Cristian-Jacques. Messerschmitt Bf 109. Caraktère. 2016.

Ministerio de Defensa.

Ministerio de Defensa. Aviones militares españoles.1986.

Peczkowski, Robert. Messerschmitt Bg-109G. Mushroom Model Publications. 2000.

Pérez San Emeterio, Carlos. Aviones para después de una guerra. Enciclopedia de la Aviación Militar Española. Editorial Quirón.

Pérez San Emeterio, Carlos. Los Messers del Ala 7, en revista Fuerza Aérea Clásica nº1. 1999.

Pérez San Emeterio, Carlos. Vicisitudes de los Buchones y sus pilotos.

Revista Aeroplano nº 29. 100 años de la Aviación Militar Española. IHCA. 2011.

Sánchez Méndez, José. La aviación militar española: una historia corta pero de gran intensidad. Arbor CLXXI, 674 (febrero 2002), 187-216.

Simón Calero, Julián; Sanz-Aránguez Sanz. Los cohetes en el INTA. Instituto Nacional de Técnica Aeroespacial "Esteban Terradas". Octubre 2012.

Yanis Velasco, Federico; Pérez Saguero, Carlos. La Escuela Superior del Aire 1939-1999. Revista Aeroplano 2016, nº 34.

www.defensa.com/ayer-noticia/la-hispano-aviacion

www.warbirdphotographs.com

www.jaon.es/batallainglaterra/batallainglaterra.htm

www.carlosalonsoaviationart.com

www.apave-es.org/aviones/cazas/me109/me109.php

www.zweiterweltkrieg.org

www.asisbiz.com

www. Wikipedia.org

The HA-1112K1L or C.4J (denomination of this aircraft in the Spanish Air Force) was popularly known as Tripala "(three bladed) only when its successor the four bladed HA-1112 M1L appeared. This survivor from the 65 HA-1112K1L manufactured is conserved in the Spanish Museum of Aeronautics and Astronautics was based during its career in Tablada, Morón, Torrejón de Ardoz and León between 1952 and 1955. It was delivered to the Air Museum in May 1971 and its preservation is superb. [By courtesy of Juan M González]

C.4J-10 (94-28) was saved from being scrapped by being sent to the Air Museum. When his picture was taken, it was still in a hangar at Cuatro Vientos airfield in the late 70s, before becoming one of the stars of the Air Museum. The HA-1112K1L (C.4J) were painted a medium bluish gray and their numbers in the fuselage were black. [Courtesy of Juan Arráez]

The C.4K-114 (471-39) still waiting for its wings in Rockcliffe Canada Aviation Museum. Since 1959, the possibility of changing the color of the painting of the Wing 7 Buchones began to be evaluated, and between 1962-1963 they went from having a cobalt blue color to having a finish in natural metal upper surfaces and light blue undersides. [Public domain by aeroprints.com]

Beautiful picture of a flight of several Wing 7 Buchones during a training flight. The last Bf 109 offspring were at least as elegant in the sky as their comrades made in Germany. The bulge of the radiocompass in the underside of the fuselage is appreciated. [Courtesy of Juan Arráez]

Among the old types of aircraft that were sent to the Sidi Ifni war were the HA-1112M1L, the Ju 52 (C.A.S.A. 352), the C.A.S.A. 2111 or the T-6 Texan two-seater trainers, although at that time Spain already had the North American F-86 Sabre. In the photograph we can see a Spanish made C.A.S.A 2111 from the Spanish Air Force. [Public Domain by Curimedia photography]

A Spanish made Ju 52 (C.A.S.A.352) in Luftwaffe markings (without swastica) belonging to EADS (Airbus). [Public Domain by Kogo Gfdl]

A Spanish made He 111 with Merlin 500-29 engines in 1975, denominated B.2I in the Spanish Air Force. Despite being an old aircraft, the proud bomber fulfilled its duty well during its war missions in the Sidi Ifni war. [Public Domain by Alexander Buschorn]

Among the different types of aircraft that were sent to the Sidi Ifni war were the HA-1112M1L, the Ju 52, the C.A.S.A. 2111 and the two seat trainers T-6 Texan, even though at that time Spain already had the North American F-86 Sabre. In the picture we can see a restaured and flyable Texan in Spanish markings. [Public Domain by Marostegui]

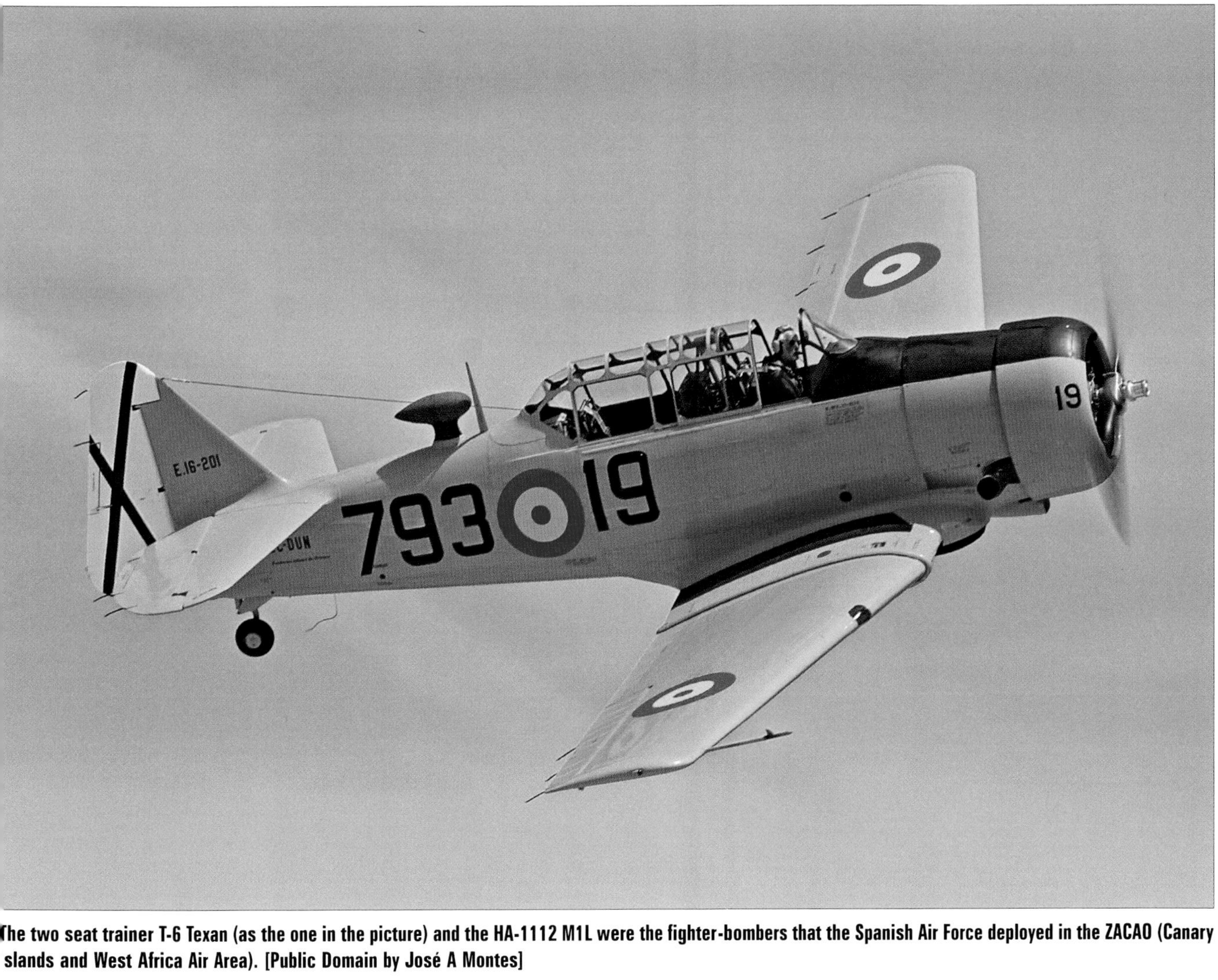

The two seat trainer T-6 Texan (as the one in the picture) and the HA-1112 M1L were the fighter-bombers that the Spanish Air Force deployed in the ZACAO (Canary Islands and West Africa Air Area). [Public Domain by José A Montes]

The color in which the Buchones were painted since they began their story in the Spanish Air Force at its base in El Copero, was the cobalt blue or Peugeot blue. In this photograph we see a HA-1112 M1L belonging to the 72 Fighter-bomber Tactical Squadron, because it shows its spinner painted yellow black split. [Courtesy of Warbirds]

One HA-1112 M1L C.4K and a Texan lined up in Son San Juan airport. The HA-1112 M1L belonged to the 72 Fighter-bomber Tactical Squadron because the spinner is painted black and yellow. [Courtesy of Juan Arráez]

With the signing of the cooperation agreements with the USA signed on September 24, 1953, the USA began to supply modern aircraft to Spain, such as Lockheed_T-33 (in the photograph in Spanish markings) that arrived in Spain in April, 1954. [Public Domain by Darz Mol]

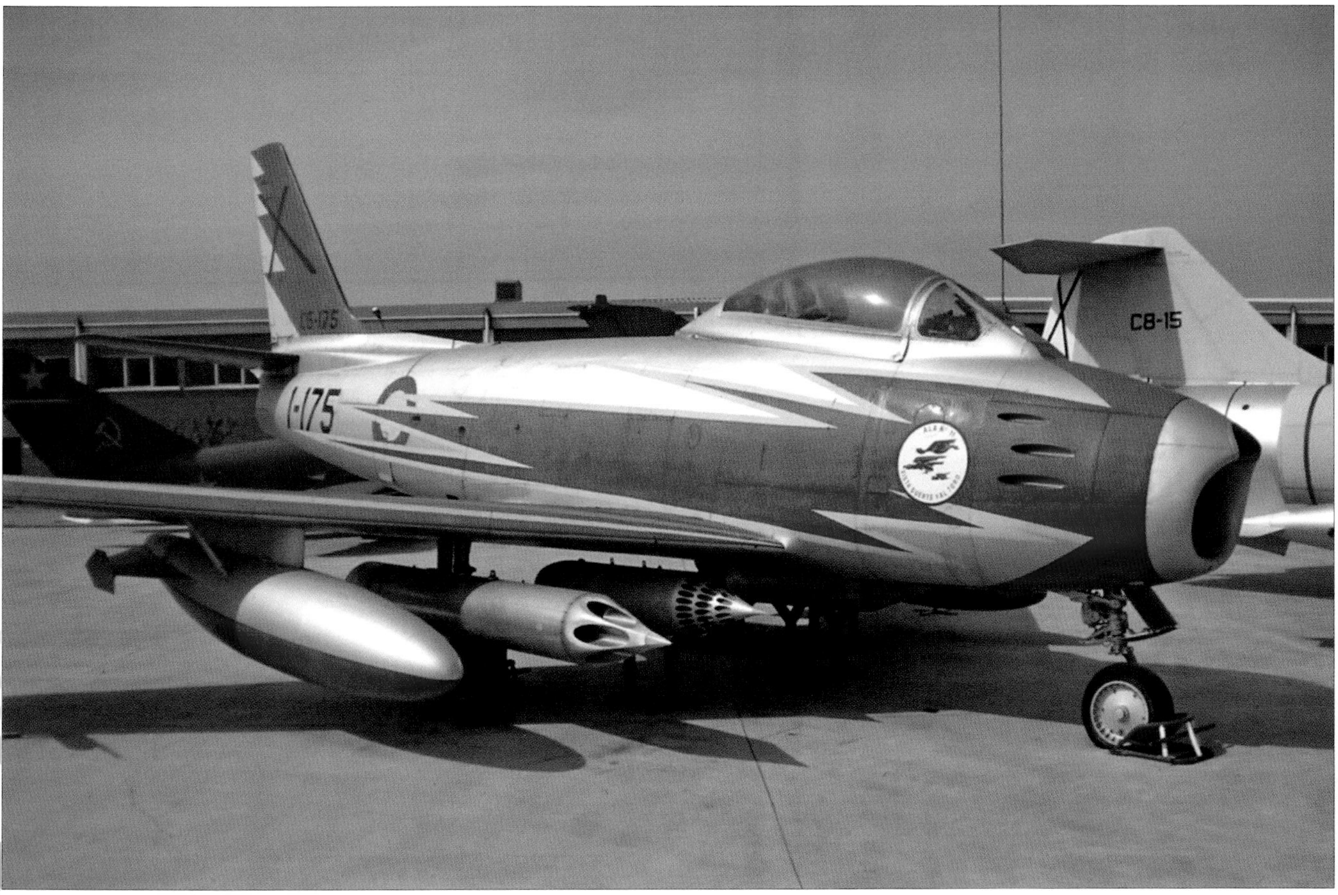

On June 30, 1955, the first F-86F "Sabre" jet arrived at Getafe (Madrid) marking a milestone in the history of Spanish Aviation. This jet was contemporary for a few months (until November 19, 1965) with the HA-1112 M1L in the Spanish Air Force. [Public Domain by Garrapata]

Another jet that was contemporary with the HA-1112 M1L in the Spanish Air Force was the F-104G "Starfighter" that arrived in January 1965. The F-104G of the photo is in the Air Museum. [Public Domain by Garrapata]

HA-1109 K in Luftwaffe camouflage for the "Battle of Britain" movie ground scenes. This aircraft was modified deleting the air intakes in both sides of the under nose and bearing the swastica in the tail. [Courtesy of Juan Arráez]

A Spanish "Luftwaffe Schwarm" waiting for the next take off. Four HA-1112 M1Ls lined up during the filming of the "Battle of Britain" movie. [By JM Ochoa via JM González]

A "Luftwaffe Rotte" flying high in May 1968 during the training for the filming of the "Battle of Britain" movie. [By JM Ochoa via JM González]

HA-1112 M1L "yellow 15" in Luftwaffe markings was one of the 28 Buchones that Spanish Air Force agreed to sell in order to film the "Battle of Britain" movie. [Courtesy of Warbirds]

Scramble, scramble! Several Buchones are ready to take off to attack British aircraft in the "Battle of Britain" movie. [Courtesy of Warbirds]

Also the black men worked on the HA-1112 M1L in order to allow them to fly again in the "Battle of Britain" movie. [Courtesy of Warbirds]

A One HA-1112 M1L "rotte" is ready to land in the Tablada airbase that is plenty of activity in the "Battle of Britain" movie. [Courtesy of Warbirds]

Pauke, pauke! A HA-1112 M1L flight looking for their foes in the Andalusian sky during the "Battle of Britain" movie. [Courtesy of Warbirds]

Superb picture of a Luftwaffe airbase in the "Battle of Britain" movie. The film's producer not only negotiated the acquisition of the aircraft, but also agreed that they would be piloted mainly by the most experienced pilots from the Wing 7 (Spanish Air Force). [Courtesy of Warbirds]

The underside of a Buchón was very similar to the underside of the Bf 109 "Battle of Britain" movie; perhaps the exhaust stubs allow us to differentiate them. Important modifications had to be made to the Buchón to make them resemble Messerschmitt Bf 109 Es. [Courtesy of Warbirds]

In this picture we can see one of the important modifications made to the HA-1112 M1L to make them resemble Messerschmitt Bf 109 Es for the "Battle of Britain" movie. The horizontal tail plans were props by struts, since the Bf 109 Fs, the tail plans had no struts. [Courtesy of Warbirds]

A Buchón in Luftwaffe markings has damaged a Spitfire that try to fly away during the filming of the "Battle of Britain" movie while 4 Buchones are looking the combat. [Courtesy of Warbirds]

The Buchones during the filming of the "Battle of Britain" movie received fictional Luftwaffe units' camouflages and markings. In the picture a HA-1112 M1L flight flying towards their aim. [Courtesy of Warbirds]

One of the four bladed HA-1112 M1L in Luftwaffe markings rests in Tablada airfield after the filming of the "Battle of Britain" movie in Tablada in 1968. In this picture we can see the right opening and low trapezoidal wing surface. [By JM Ochoa via JM González]

After finishing the filming of the "Battle of Britain" movie, some planes that were static and that had not flown in the film were abandoned. Picture taken in Tablada airbase in 1969. In the background we can see another Bucher and two B.2I stored too. [By courtesy of Juan M González]

Another HA-1112 M1L in Luftwaffe markings (this one in three blade configuration) abandoned in open air in Tablada airbase 1969 after completing the filming of the "Battle of Britain" movie. [By courtesy of Juan M González]

The same HA-1112 M1L from last picture showing us the elegant profile of this aircraft. It's noteworthy the long eyebrow shaped bulges in the upper engine cover and the reason why this aircraft was called unofficially by the workers of the Hispano Aviation as "Buchón" or "Pouter" in English. [By courtesy of Juan M González]

A lonely HA-1112 K1L in Luftwaffe markings because the "Battle of Britain" movie, waiting in the airport. Thanks to this film, nowadays several HA-1112 M1L and a HA-1112 M4L still can be seen flying. [By Fernando Llorente via JM González]

Facade of Hispano Aviation factory in San Jacinto Street 102 in the neighborhood of Triana (Seville) today. [Picture taken by the author]

Panel on the facade of the Hispano Aviación factory in Seville, remembering that it was placed there between 1943-1972. The history of the Hispano Aviación continued with the manufacture of various aircraft among which the fabulous Ha-200 "Saeta" designed in 1955 by Willy Messerschmitt (it was the first jet manufactured in Spain), until that in 1971 was absorbed by its "brother" Construcciones Aeronáuticas Sociedad Anónima (CASA). [Picture taken by the author]

Close-up of the shield on the top of the facade of the Hispano Aviación factory in Sevilla. Its predecessor "La Hispano-Suiza, Fábrica de Automóviles, S.A.", which from 1915 began to build aviation engines. [Picture taken by the author]

An flyable Spanish made four bladed HA-1112 M1L in Luftwaffe markings (swastika included) nowadays. Fortunately, there are several Buchones that are still flyables. [By courtesy of Juan M González]

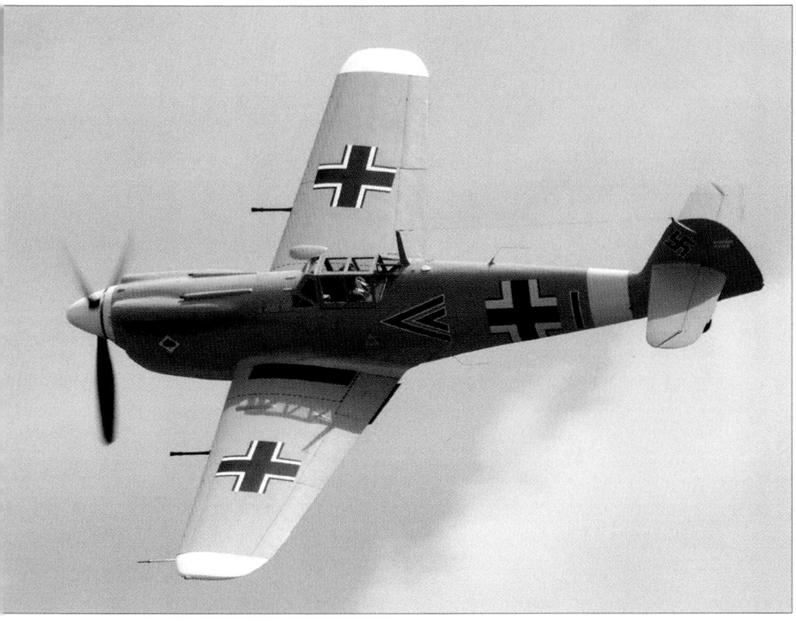

Picture taken in July 1, 2012. During the Flying Legends airshow (Duxford), this desert scheme camuflaged HA-1112 M1L (G-AWHE) shows its elegant silhouette. [Courtesy of Ricardo Sanabria]

During the Flying Legends airshow in 2011 (Duxford), the "stars" were the HA-1112 M1Ls. The Buchones in Luftwaffe markings were the feared enemies of the RAF aircraft. [Courtesy of Ricardo Sanabria]

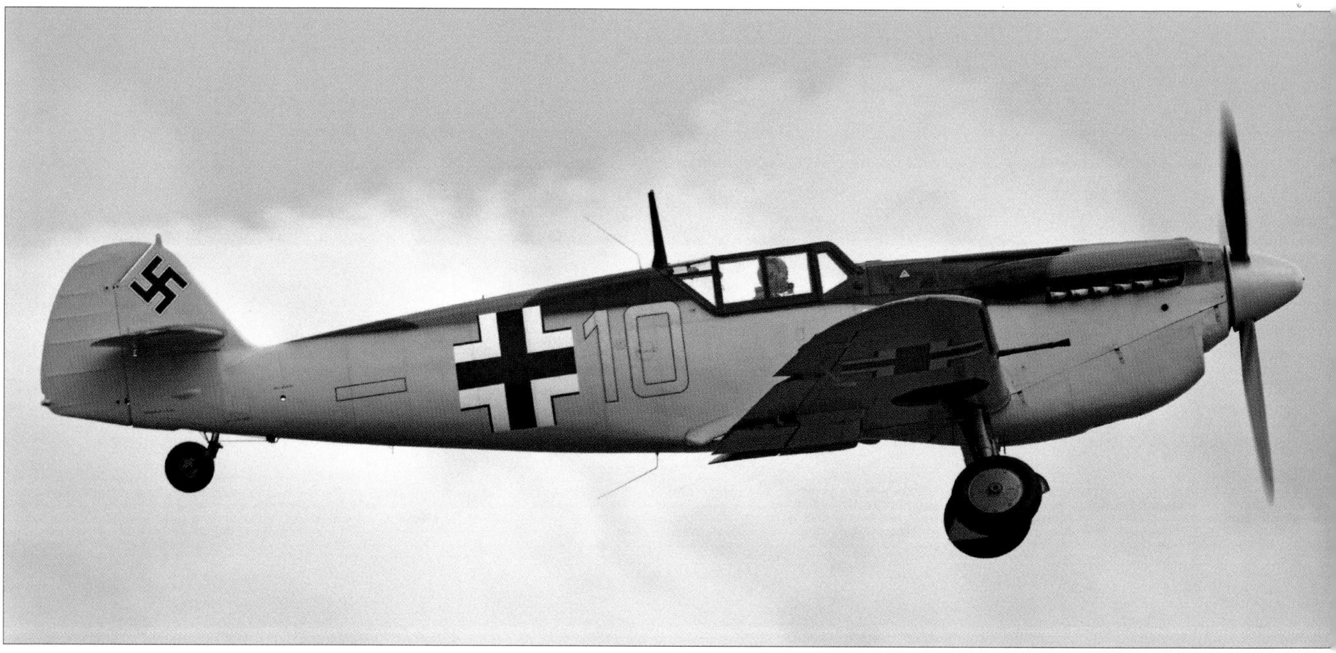

Another picture of the HA-1112 M1L "yellow 10" (G-BWUE) resembling a Bf 109 with great success in airshows. [Public Domain by Alan Wilson]

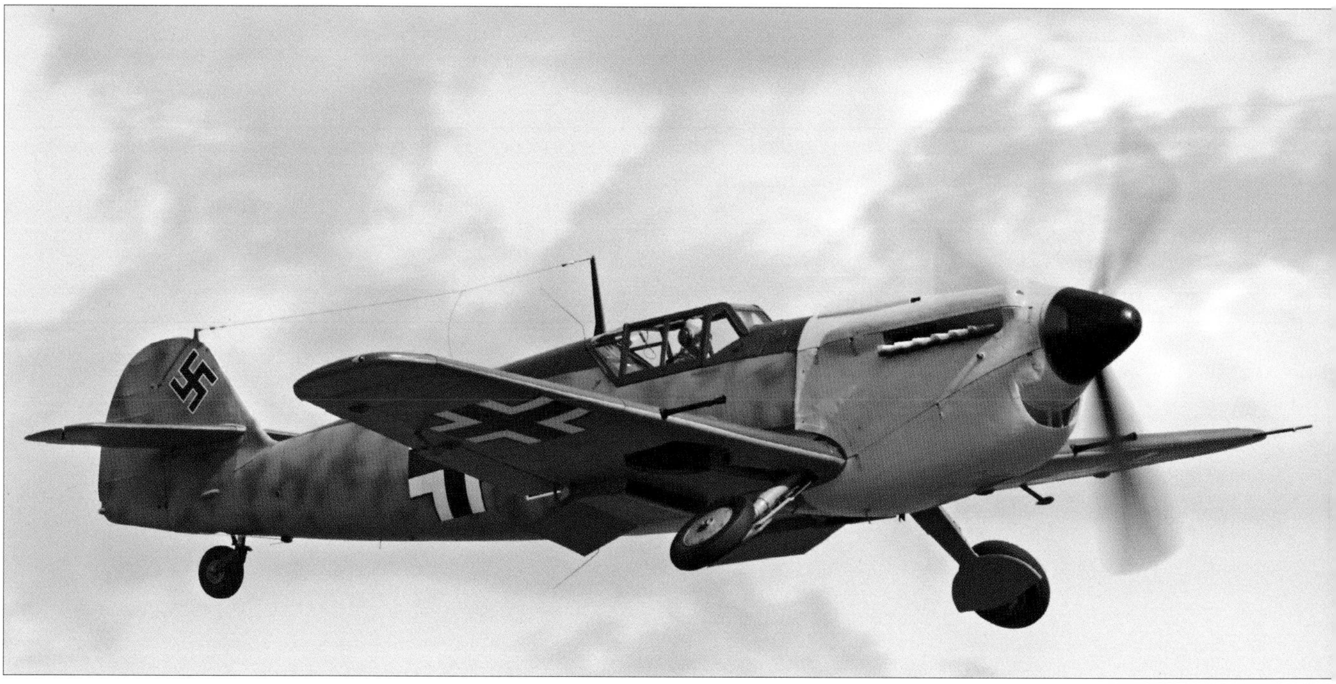

This HA-1112 M1L (C.4K-102) is now Duxford based and is operated by ARCo. [Public Domain by Alan Wilson from Stilton, Peterborough, Cambs, UK]

In this picture, two HA-1112 M1Ls fly very close. It's noteworthy that the Buchón in the background bears the swastica in its tail, but the Buchón in the foreground bears only four black lines. The reason is that in Germany nazi symbols are forbidden, but the England based use the swastica. [Courtesy of Ricardo Sanabria]

Since the "Battle of Britain" film in 1968 we had not seen 3 109 (HA-1112 M1L) flying together. The picture was taken on July 9, 2011 in Flying Legends airshow and we can see the old C.4K-31, C.4K-102 and C.4K-169. [Courtesy of Ricardo Sanabria]

A "rotte" of HA-1112 M1L fly in an airshow. The Buchón to the right has the swastica in the tail, but the other Buchón not. [Public Domain by Tony Hisgett from Birmingham, UK]

This shot shows the cockpit of a restored HA-1112 M1L (G-BOML), where we can see the instrument panel, rudder pedals, side consoles and control column. This Bf 109 G-2 derivative still makes people enjoy in airshows and Museums. [Public Domain by Towpilot]

After its long restoration, the C.4K-31 flew again on May 6 and was one of the stars of the Flying Legends 2011, just with the C.4K-102 and C.4K-169. We can appreciate the good state appearance of the airplane after being restored. [Courtesy of Ricardo Sanabria]

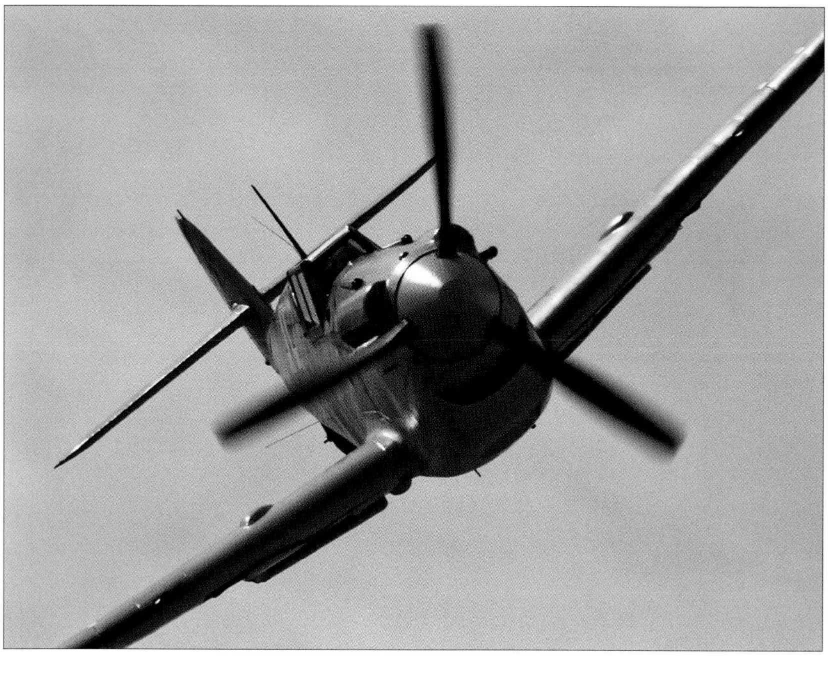

Impressive photograph of an HA-1112 M1L "attacking". The author of the photo says that the Buchón flew only 5 meter over his head; Surely it was an unforgettable experience. This picture of the "Yellow 10" taken on September 5, 2010, was the 3rd price in the photo contest AIRE. [Courtesy of Ricardo Sanabria]

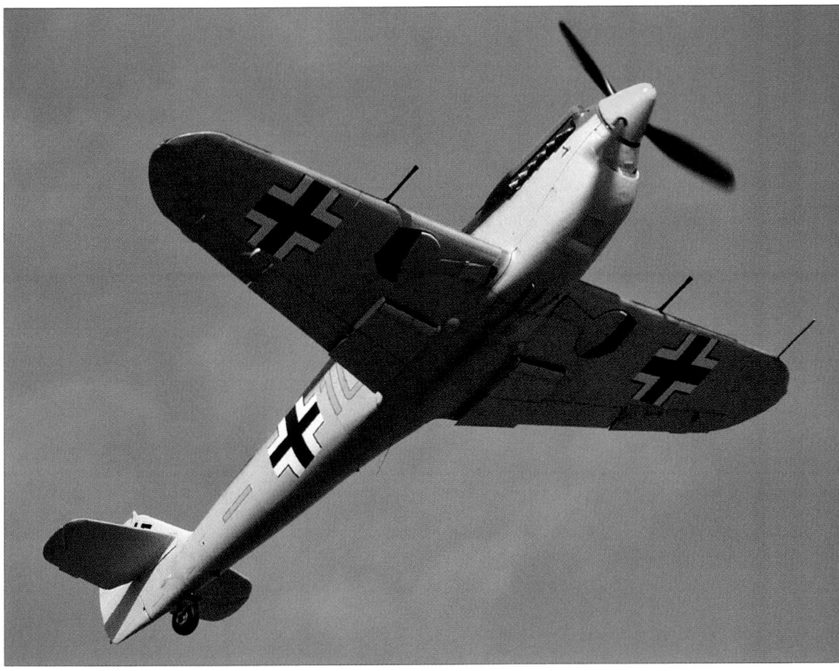

The HA-1112 M1L (G-BWUE) is showing us the underside where the resemblance to Bf 109 is almost complete. The picture was taken on September 5, 2010. [Courtesy of Ricardo Sanabria]

To celebrate the 70th anniversary of the Battle of Britain, the HA-1112 M1L (C.4K-102) was "dressed" again in the same Luftwaffe markings that were used in the "Battle of Britain" film. Picture taken on May 22, 2010 in La Ferte Alais. [Courtesy of Ricardo Sanabria]

The beautiful HA-1112 M1L (G-BWUE) "red 1" taxiing in Duxford airfield during Flying Legends 2006. [Courtesy of Ricardo Sanabria]

Another picture of the HA-1112 M1L (G-BWUE) "red 1" during Flying Legends airshow 2006. Only a few of the HA-1112M1Ls are flyable, but most of the HA-1112M1L and HA-1112K1L that we can see nowadays are on static display in aeronautical museums or belong to companies or individuals that with their effort have managed to keep them in storage and in some cases it's possible that they could take to the air again someday. [Courtesy of Ricardo Sanabria]

The two seat trainer HA-1112 M4L (C.4K-112) still in the same Luftwaffe markings used in the "Battle of Britain" film. This aircraft was before one of the two HA-1110 K1L manufactured. [Courtesy of Ricardo Sanabria]

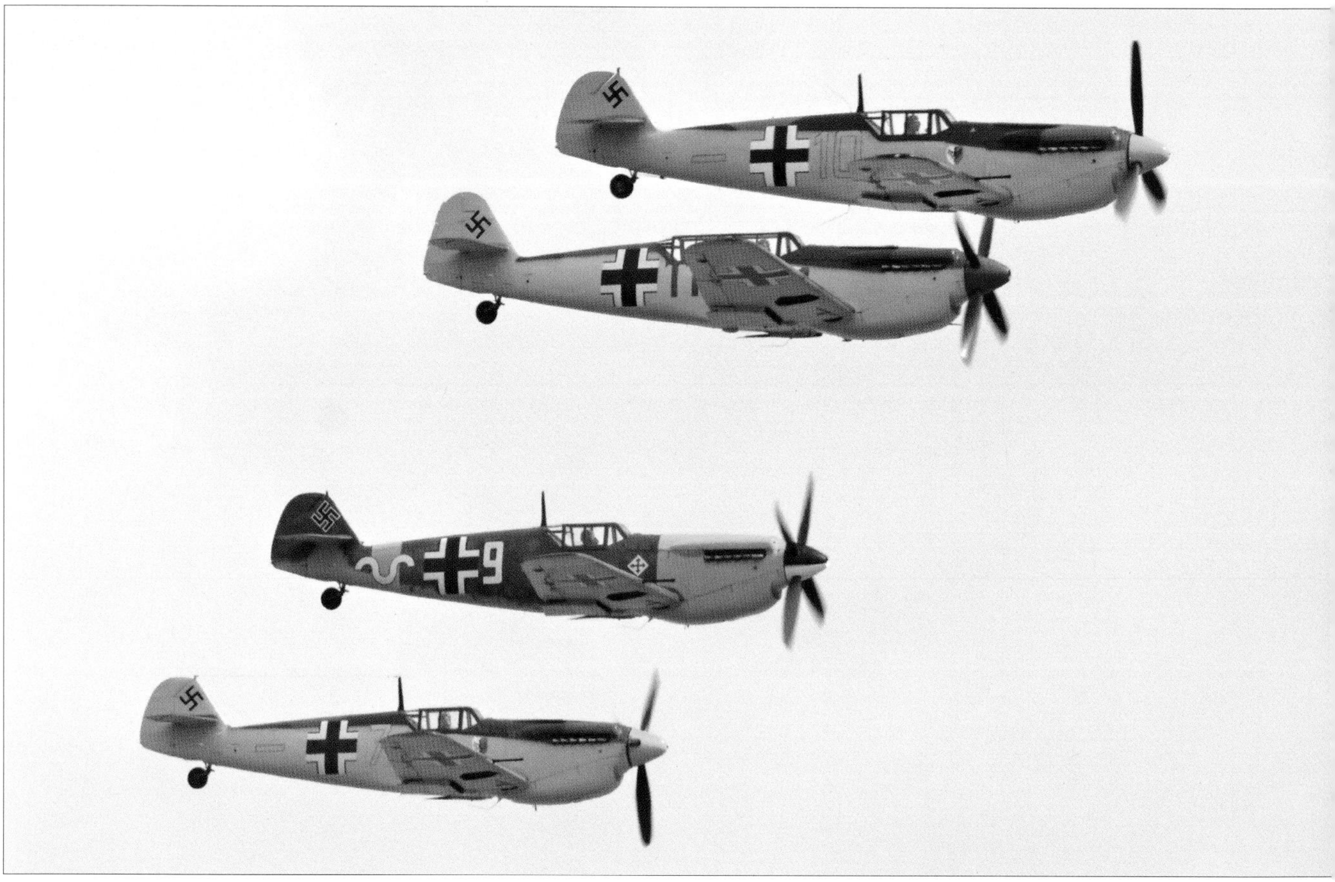

The 2018 Flying Legends Airshow in Duxford included no less than three HA-1112 M1Ls and one HA-1112 M4L. From top to bottom: "Yellow 10" (G-AWHK and before C.4K-102), two seat "Red 11" (G-AWHC and before C.4K-112), "White 9" (G-AWHH and before C.4K-105) and "Yellow 7" (G-AWHM and before C.4K-99). [Public Domain by Alan Wilson from Stilton, Peterborough, Cambs, UK]

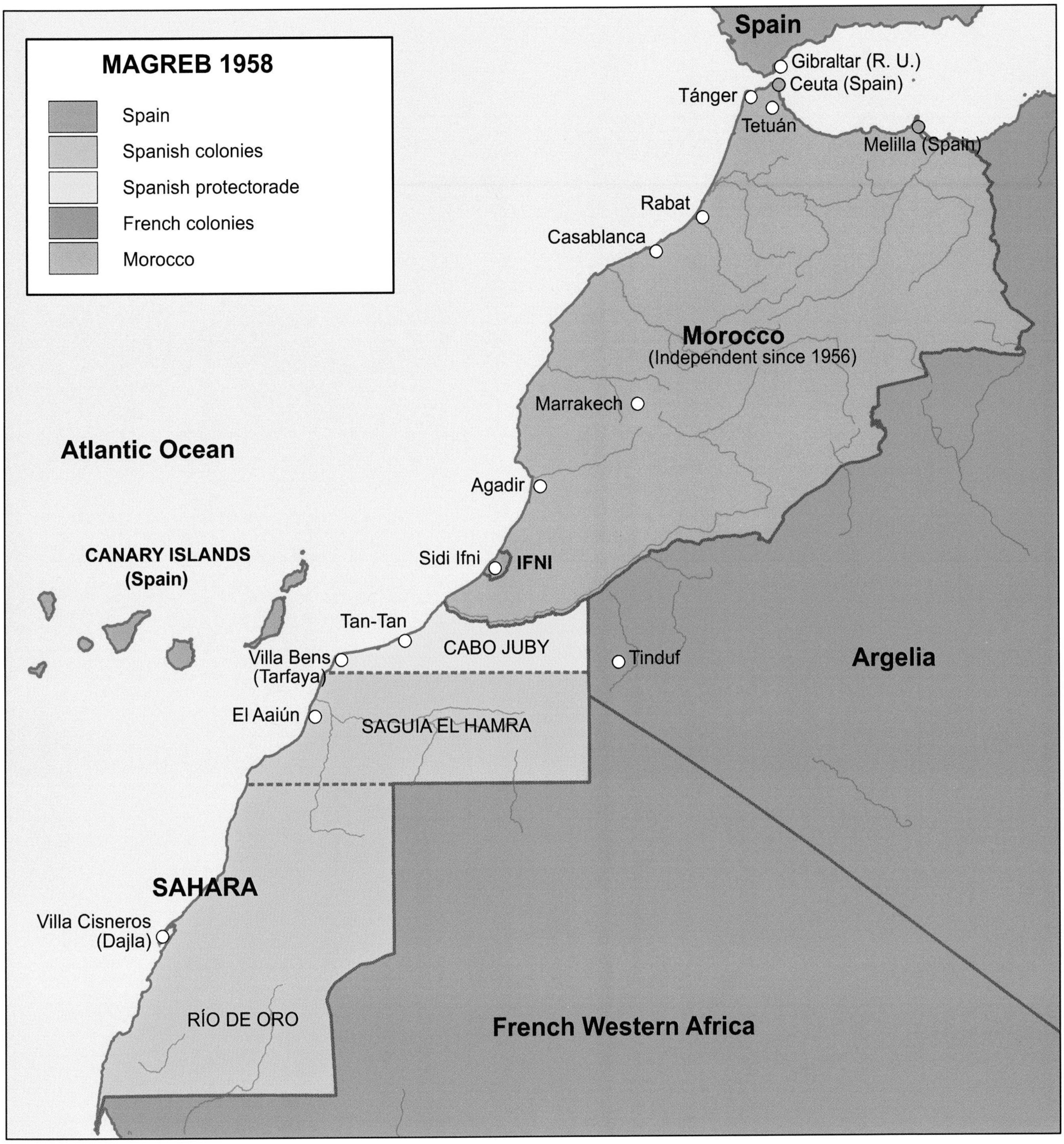

This map shows the geographical situation of the Magreb in 1958. It´s easy to understand the difficult communication between Spain and its territories in Northern and Western Africa and Canary Islands. [Public Domain by Shadowxfox from TUBS work with modifications]

Painted by Arkadiusz Wróbel

Messerschmitt Bf 109 E-3 6-130. El Prat de Llobregat (Barcelona), December 1940. At the beginning of 1939, the J/88 of the Condor Legion was equipped with Messerschmitt Bf 109 E-1 and E-3. This "Emil" is one of the Messerschmitts that remained in Spain after the Spanish Civil War and still bears typical war badges as the black round badges on both sides of the fuselage with a white Falange´s symbol (Yoke and Arrows) or the black circle with white diagonal cross insignia in the underwings. It´s noteworthy in the rudder the black St. Andrew´s Cross painted on a white background; and in the tail we can see a badge consisting in a white circle with three birds in the middle (a hawk, a bustard and a blackbird) and the phrase "Vista, suerte y al toro" that means "Sight, luck and 'nut up'. On December 7, 1940, during an aeronautical exhibition in El Prat de Llobregat this aircraft crashed.

Messerschmitt Bf 109 F-4 C.4F-145 / 23-51 23° Regimiento de Caza. Reus (Tarragona), 1943. The aircraft still is painted in desert camouflage scheme, later the Spanish Bf 109 Fs changed to a three colors splinter camouflage. It bears the national red-yellow-red cockade (a circle with the three colors of the Spanish national flag: red in the outside ring - yellow in the middle ring - red in the inner disc) on the wings and both sides of the fuselage. The codes were two numbers ahead of and behind the Spanish roundel on the fuselage. In the rudder the black St. Andrew´s Cross is painted on a white background.

Painted by Arkadiusz Wróbel

Hispano Aviación HA-1109 J1L or Me 109 J. Tablada (Sevilla). Summer, 1945. The aircraft was a Messerschmitt Bf 109 G-2 fuselage fitted with a HS12-Z89 engine. The engine overheating observed during the aircraft trials was tried to solve with the installation of a large radiator in the lower part of the engine, but it was not definitely avoided. Its maiden flight was in 1945 and after several tests the results were very disappointing. The HA-1109 J1L bears the Spanish cockade on the wings and both sides of the fuselage and the black St. Andrew´s Cross on a white background in the rudder. The two tones grey camouflage was not continued in others aircraft.

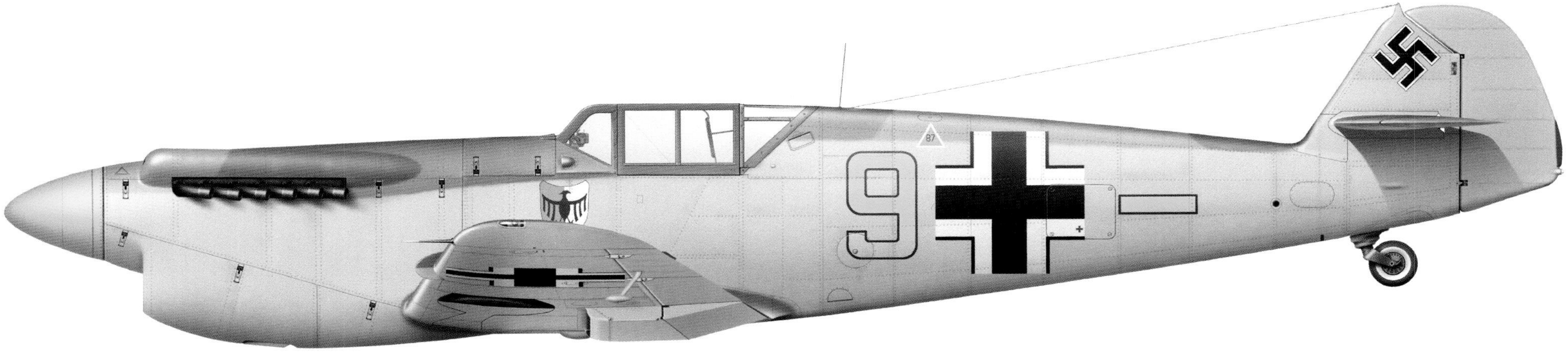

Hispano Aviación HA-1112 M1L (yellow 9) Duxford (UK). Summer, 1968. As the Phoenix, the Buchón reborned from its ashes. The last Buchones (plural for Buchón) were written off in 1965 (although still in flyable condition) but during 1967-1968 several HA-1112 took part in the British film "Battle of Britain" thanks to the Ejército del Aire that agreed to sell 18 flyable, 6 taxi-capable and 4 static Buchones for the film. This aircraft resembles the Bf 109 E that fought during the Battle of Britain and belongs to the Yellow Staffeln. The camuflage scheme is similar to the Bf 109s that fought the Battle of Britain; and the swastica is painted on the tail. The Unit crest painted (a black eagle on a White-blue shield) in the fuselage under the canopy didn´t belong to a real Luftwaffe unit. Note that the aircraft have false antenne and mock-ups on MG FF cannon and MG 17 machine guns.

Painted by Arkadiusz Wróbel

Hispano Aviación HA-1112 M1L C.4K-32 / 36-408 Ala Mixta 36. Gando, Islas Canarias (España). 1963. In October of 1962, the Spanish Air Force expeditionary units in Western Africa were based at the Gando airport (Canary Islands) under the name Ala Mixta 36 (Mixed Wing 36). The HA-1112 M1Ls were deployed in the 364 Squadron. The 364 Squadron was disbanded possibly in August 1964, after two years and 805 flight hours since it was created. Between 1962-1963 the Buchones changed the cobalt blue camuflage to aluminum color in the aircraft upper areas and light blue in the lower areas. In order to avoid the dazzle of the pilot, the nose panel was painted in dark green. The spinner is painted in yellow and white. This Buchón bears the Spanish cockade on the wings and both sides of the fuselage and the black St. Andrew´s Cross on a white background in the rudder. The bulge under the aircraft is the radiocompass. This aircraft crashed while landing in October 22, 1963; then it was written off.

Hispano Aviación HA-1112 M1L C.4K-154 /441-4 441 Escuadrón. Torrejón de Ardoz (Madrid). Early 60´s. In March 29, 1961 this aircraft was destined to the Flight Experimentation Group (bearing code number 64-4) where several tests were done and later was deployed to the 441 Escuadrón, changing the code number. This aircraft shows us the cobalt blue (blue nº 9) camuflage so typical of the Buchones. The HA-1112M1Ls had the spinners painted split black and red or yellow or white during their service time in the Spanish Air Force; this time is black-red. This Buchón bears the Ala 7 crest in the engine cowling: a white diving pelican over a black 7. As usual in the Ejército del Aire, the Spanish cockade is painted on the wings and both sides of the fuselage and the black St. Andrew´s Cross on a white background in the rudder. Above the code number in the tail [illegible]

Painted by Arkadiusz Wróbel

Hispano Aviación HA-1112 M1L MI-V (ex C.4K-171, and nowadays G-AWHJ) Polish Squadron. Duxford (UK). Summer, 1968. A very strange badges and camuflage for a Buchón, but everything has an explanation. When the "Battle of Britain" film was getting ready it became obvious the lack of airworthy Hurricanes, so three Buchones were painted temporarily over to resemble Polish RAF Hurricanes, and they were named Hurrischmitt. The aircraft shows a standard RAF camuflage overall and Polish insignia on the engine cowling. "Battle of Britain" film definitely gave to the HA-1112M1L world fame and revealed the potential of the Spanish Buchón in the movies.

Hispano Aviación HA-1112 M1L C.4K-118 /7-15 Ala Mixta 36. Gando, Islas Canarias (España). 1963. This aircraft is one of the Buchones deployed in Canary Island during early 60´s and it still retain the 72 Squadron code number. Its camuflage has aluminum color in the aircraft upper areas and light blue in the lower areas. As usual in the Ejército del Aire, the Spanish cockade is painted on the wings and both sides of the fuselage and the black St. Andrew´s Cross on a white background in the rudder. The spinners in the 72 Squadron were painted split black and yellow. Above the code number in the tail, we can see the Hispano Aviación badge: a flying stork close to the words Hispano Aviación.

Painted by Arkadiusz Wróbel

Hispano Aviación HA-1112 M1L C.4K-99 /7-77 Ala 7. El Copero (Sevilla). Early 60´s. The aircraft is painted in aluminum color in the upper areas and light blue in the lower areas. As usual the Spanish cockade is painted on the wings and both sides of the fuselage and the black St. Andrew´s Cross on a white background in the rudder. This Buchón bears the Ala 7 crest in the engine cowling: a white diving pelican over a black 7 and above the code number in the tail, we can see the Hispano Aviación badge: a flying stork close to the words Hispano Aviación. It´s noteworthy that the spinner is painted in four colors, the outside being white, the yellow in the middle, the red inside and the primer black). Notable is the armament: 20 mm HS.404 cannon in the wing and underwing launch rails for 80 mm unguided Oerlikon rockets.

Hispano Aviación HA-1112 M1L C.4K-17 /71-0 (EL COPERO) 71 Escuadrón de caza-bombardeo. El Copero (Sevilla). January 1958. This was the aircraft of the 71 Fighter-bomber Tactical Squadron boss, major Comas Altadill. Flying this aircraft he led 14 pilots on January 30, 1958 from Sevilla to Spanish Western Africa during the Sidi Ifni war. The aircraft shows the drop tank that allowed them to reach their destination. The drop tanks were designed for the ferry flight and not to be used in combat missions. The bulge under the aircraft is the radiocompass Lear ADF-14B. The aircraft is painted in cobalt blue (oficial name color nº9 NH-36-08-01). It´s noteworthy that the spinner is painted in three colors, the outside being white, the red in the middle and the black inside. In the engine cowling is painted an eight-pointed white star (only the chief of the unit has this badge) and close to the spinner the words "El Copero". As usual the Spanish cockade is on the wings and both sides of the fuselage and the black St. Andrew´s Cross on a white background in the rudder. Above the code number in the tail, we can see the Hispano Aviación badge: a flying stork close to the words Hispano Aviación.